GEORGE PLUMPTRE

The Water Garden

STYLES, DESIGNS AND VISIONS

Photographs by Hugh Palmer

With 267 illustrations 174 in color

THAMES AND HUDSON

PHOTOGRAPHER'S DEDICATION
To my sons,
Leander and Ged

© 1993 Thames and Hudson Ltd,
London

Text © 1993 George Plumptre

Special photography
© 1993 Hugh Palmer

First published in the United States of
America in 1993 by Thames and
Hudson Inc., 500 Fifth Avenue,
New York, New York 10110

Library of Congress Catalog Card
Number 92-82077

Printed and bound in Singapore

Contents

Half title page *A group of dolphin spouts.*
Frontispiece *Fountain at Folly Farm, Berkshire, designed by Sir Edwin Lutyens.*
Title page Nymphaea marliacea purpurea.
This lion spout (left) makes a dramatic source for a shallow water staircase at Brook Cottage, Oxfordshire.

IN THE ANCIENT WORLD *water fulfilled both practical and symbolic roles; once controlled and contained in channels and basins, it could give both life and aesthetic pleasure. Diverted from the Tigris, Euphrates and the Nile and then distributed and stored, water made possible the gardens which, from the earliest periods, were the first representations of man's desire for tranquil and beautiful surroundings to his home, complementing a house or palace as a representation of success and grandeur and offering the luxuries of shade from the sun, the production of fruit and flowers and respite from the harsh toil of human existence. Water was the element which made the creation of the garden possible; in various manifestations throughout the history of garden design, it has continued to provide essential life and interest.*

*Formality and movement at
Nymphenburg, Bavaria.*

Reflections

*O*ne of the great qualities which water brings to the garden is reflection, expanding and emphasizing both architectural and natural features. In all the examples illustrated here a whole new, subtle, mysterious dimension has been added to the garden, from the reflections of architecture and sculpture at Buscot Park, Oxfordshire (right) and Knightshayes, Devon (opposite), to the harmonious combination of water with snow-capped boulders and pine trees at Machida, Tokyo (below right) and the tranquil formalism of the Chehel Sutun in Isfahan (below).

Movement A *powerful sense of dramatic motion is the overriding effect in both the fountain at Waddesden Manor, Buckinghamshire (above) and the cascade at the Palazzo Reale, Caserta (opposite). The combination of animated figures – at Waddesden the Triton fountain and at the Palazzo Reale Diana and her nymphs – and water in motion has traditionally been used to create the most dramatic focal points of the water garden.*

Symmetry

The magnificent Bassin d'Apollon (above) acts as a focal point between the canal and the Tapis Vert along the main axis of the garden of Versailles. At La Mortola, on the island of Ischia, the formality of the narrow rill and fountain (below right) is softened by luxuriant planting on both sides. Harold Peto's water garden at Buscot Park, Oxfordshire (left) perfectly illustrates the harmony between a formal water garden and more natural surroundings.

Planting The *formal arrangement of plants enhances the architectural effects of a pool and fountain at Meadowbank Farm, Pennsylvania (above); at Coombe Wood, Surrey (opposite) trees and shrubs increase the 'natural' effect of the pool and fountain.*

Water and the Garden

1

THE NECESSITY of water and the most effective means of its transport and containment were fundamental influences on the overall design of the earliest Egyptian gardens. Straight rectangular canals and channels, through which water could be raised up from the river by a system of dams and sluices, combined with rectangular shapes for storage pools, inspired the emergence of a symmetrical enclosure as the universally adopted garden plan. Probably the most decisive Egyptian invention was the *shadoof*, or well-sweep, still used today; an upright pole with a cross-arm, from one end of which hung a crude bucket for collecting water and from the other a counter-weight. Every garden had at least one *shadoof* for the easy distribution of water and this in itself influenced planting, notably in the development of close, chequer-board-pattern, square beds which maximized the efficiency of watering, a constant requirement.

It is clear from surviving descriptions and illustrations from different periods of the Egyptian kingdoms that the fundamental features of the garden changed little through the three thousand years or so from the establishment of the Old Kingdom *c.* 3000 BC to the conquest of the country by Alexander the Great in 332 BC. The essentials were water, selected trees and flowers, a vineyard and small pavilions, which were present in almost all gardens; what changed and progressed was the complexity of their arrangement. Possibly the best and most striking picture of an Egyptian garden survives in a Theban tomb thought to be the resting place of a high priest from the reign of Amenhotep III (*c.* 1411–1375 BC). Water features are of primary importance; the approach to the villa and its surrounding garden is via a formal canal of impressive length and, within the garden, four rectangular pools delineate the garden's logical sub-division into separate areas.

The gardens of the Egyptians were essentially for private enjoyment and relaxation and were therefore attractive rather than impressive. Once established as a domestic sanctuary from harsh natural surroundings, the garden became the means for Egyptians to demonstrate their love of nature in the flowers that were vital to every garden and in the pools and canals stocked with fish and water birds.

The Egyptian shadoof *(well-sweep) was one of man's first irrigation tools.*

The sound of water, seen or unseen, is one of the most interesting effects in a garden. At Shute House, Wiltshire, Geoffrey Jellicoe designed a series of descending 'harmonic' cascades, each of which produces a different musical pitch (opposite).

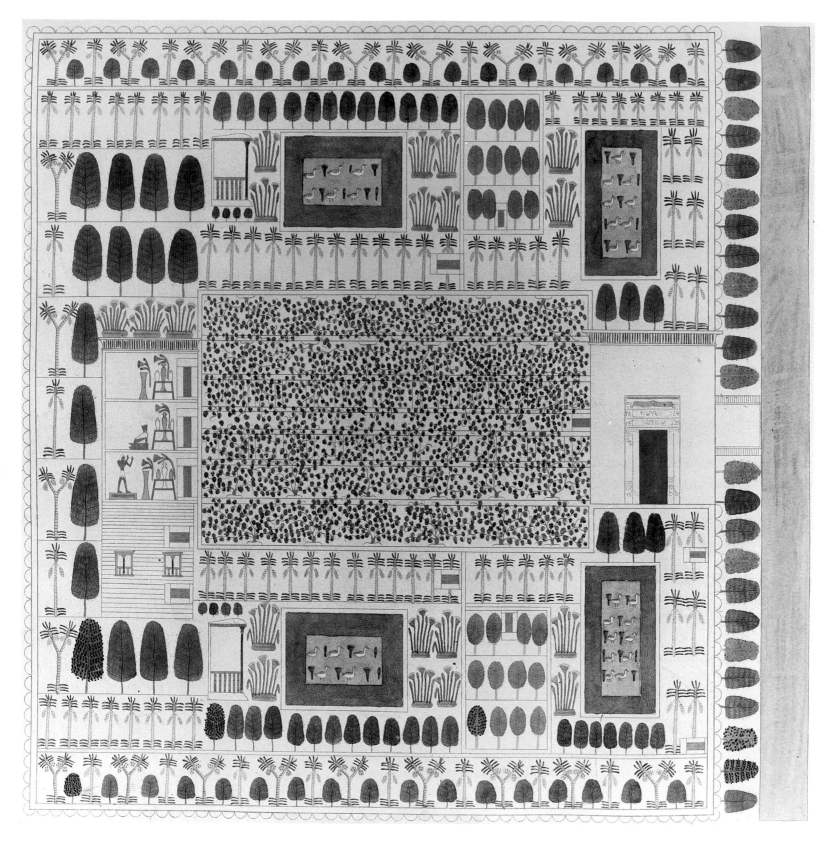

Unlike the case of Ancient Egypt, there is no surviving documentation of the gardens of Mesopotamia, the country established in the alluvial flood plain between the rivers Tigris and Euphrates. As in the case of the Nile valley, however, the evolution of all cultivation and the creation of gardens was dictated by the need to control the flood waters of the two great rivers. The annual floods, racing down from the rivers' sources in the mountains, were brief but devastating; controlling them demanded human organization on an impressive scale, which also helped to establish the city culture of the Sumerians. The flood water was channelled into large reservoirs, from which irrigation systems could be fed throughout the year. The oldest surviving carved water basin, dating from around 3000 BC, was discovered at the site of Tello, one of the cities of Mesopotamia. At Mari, another of the most important cities, a stone fountain figure dating from around 2000 BC was discovered. The figure can be considered a prototype for the kind of fountains made in gardens for thousands of years thereafter: a female goddess holding a vase into which water was piped to pour forth, symbolizing the source of all life, the ultimate creative force of the garden.

From this early control of the water supply emerged systems which in turn made possible the great hunting parks planted by the warrior Assyrians and, at the same time, the basic hydraulics which raised water up for the terraced gardens of ziggurats, most famously the Hanging Gardens of Babylon, were developed. Unfortunately, neither the great terraced gardens of Mesopotamia nor the wooded groves of Assyria survive in any form. It is clear, however, that the availability and control of water were the determining factors in the evolution of gardens and that, as a result, water assumed great symbolic importance – an importance which was continued in both Christian European gardens and in Islamic gardens. Not only was the biblical Garden of Eden similar to an ancient tree park, but it was traditionally situated in Mesopotamia. The basic principle of a paradise garden divided by the four rivers of life became the central inspiration for the Persian *chahar-bagh* whose essential form and reliance upon channels of water remained unchanged through centuries of Islamic gardens in Europe, Africa and Asia.

The creation of private gardens were much less an intrinsic part of life in Ancient Greece than, for instance, in Ancient Egypt; the culture of the country was based much more on the collective than on the individual and, in any case, the harsh terrain of much of it did not inspire the creation of luxuriant gardens. Admittedly, Homer's *Odyssey* describes the garden of Alcinous at Phaeacia and includes the passage, 'There are two

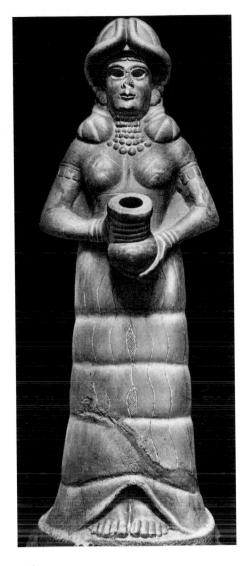

A Mesopotamian stone fountain figure, c. 2000 BC, discovered in the city of Mari.

The plan of a garden in Thebes (opposite) shows how rectangular pools acted as the main unifying factor in the gardens of Ancient Egypt, while the long tree-lined canal provided a cool, majestic approach to the garden.

The holy spring near Delphi was among the most important natural sites which inspired the gardens of Ancient Greece; it is seen here in an anonymous nineteenth-century engraving.

streams, one of them traversing the whole garden, the other passing below the threshold of the court of the great house', but elsewhere in Homer's writing and certainly until roughly the time of Epicurus (341–270 BC), the concept of a garden was most readily associated with a natural place sacred to gods and possessing a spring.

From the earliest and simplest of these revered sites, often little more than a remote wooded grove around a natural spring, were derived decorative fountains as well as grottoes and nymphaea. These were initially natural places occupied by nymphs or other deities and many centuries later incorporated into European gardens as important ornamental features.

The significance of water naturally issuing forth from the earth in springs, then, was a far greater influence upon the Ancient Greeks than, for instance, the more contemplative qualities of still pools and canals, the salient features of Egyptian gardens. One of the most sacred sites to the Muses was the fountain of Hippocrene on the slopes of Mount Helicon, created in legend by the hoof of Pegasus striking the ground and causing a natural spring to appear. The sites of springs were eventually adorned with figurative sculpture and thus elevated into elementary fountains which were introduced into all main cities. One of the earliest, in Athens, dated from between 560 and 510 BC, with water issuing from the mouths of nine bronze lions' heads. Others, especially those decorated with representations of the gods, such as the Neptune fountain in Corinth, achieved widely revered status.

Public parks and gardens became increasingly widespread features of Greek cities, especially around the periphery of the empire, towards Persia and in Egypt, where established and widely practised garden traditions exerted strong influence. In Alexandria, during the first century AD, the mathematician Hero produced his treatise, *Pneumatica*, which was to influence directly the waterworks in Italian Renaissance gardens, in particular the work of Pirro Ligorio, creator of the Villa d'Este. Hero's work included descriptions of fountains and hydraulic or mechanical water devices; his influence is exemplified by one passage in which he describes '. . . birds made to sing and be silent alternately by flowing water'.

The supreme characteristic of Roman gardens was a harmony between natural features and architecture; the role of water in achieving this was decisive. The two extremes of the Roman garden are exemplified by the Temple of Vesta at Tivoli – a favourite place of Augustus during whose reign the temple was built in 27 BC – perched on a rocky outcrop overlooking the gorge of the river Aniene, and by the intimate peristyles of the houses and villas uncovered at Pompeii, where cool colonnades enclose small gardens enlivened by fountain basins. Tivoli became perhaps the most evocative inspiration for all future romantic landscapes, but the gardens of Pompeii are marvellous examples of water bringing life to small, highly architectural and symmetrical enclosures.

The evidence preserved at Pompeii gives a clear picture of gardens either enclosed by peristyles, or taking the form of a *xystus*, a symmetrical rectangular continuation of the atrium and peristyle of the house. In both cases the central feature which emphasized the symmetry of the design was a square pool or rectangular canal, often decorated with fountains and lined on both sides with an arrangement of statues and planting.

The letters of Pliny the Younger are one of the most important sources of information about Roman gardens; two of the volumes describe the gardens at his two villas: Laurentinum beside the sea but close enough to Rome to be accessible at the end of the working day, and Tusci in the hills outside Rome on a site overlooking the upper valley of the Tiber. Pliny's own accounts give a clear picture of the layout of the latter villa and of its garden features. He describes the extensive hippodrome, enclosed by plane trees and ending in a semi-circle of closely planted cypresses, a network of paths divided by box hedges, and in another area a pattern of apple trees and obelisks. He also notes the importance of water, 'At the upper end is a semicircular bench of white marble, shaded with a vine which is trained upon four small pillars of Carystian marble. Water, gushing through several little pipes from under this bench, as if it were pressed out by the weight of the persons who repose themselves upon it, falls into a stone cistern underneath, from whence it is received into a fine polished marble basin, so artfully contrived that it is always full without ever overflowing ... Opposite this is a fountain which is incessantly emptying and filling, for the water which it throws up to a great height falling back into it, is by means of connected openings returned as fast as it is received ...'

The most renowned horticultural survivor from the Roman Empire was the garden of Hadrian's villa at Tivoli. The most monumental of the water features was the rectangular canal or pool which formed the centrepiece of the Pecile or hippodrome (so named, it is thought, because it is a copy of the Stoa Poikile in Athens); an idea of the overall site is given by the fact that the porticoes of the two long sides stretched for over five hundred yards. But the variety of the villa's water features is better

This view of the temple and falls at Tivoli by Samuel Palmer (c. 1838) shows the juxtaposition of water in the landscape and architecture which Roman and, later, Renaissance Italian gardeners so admired.

*W*ater features were central to the orderly but decorative gardens of Pompeii and Herculaneum (above).

demonstrated by comparing the Marine Theatre and the Canopus – the latter probably the best preserved and best-known feature of the whole villa complex. The former was not, in fact, a theatre but a private creation of the utmost ingenuity; inside an enclosing circular wall a portico encircled a round pool with a central island only accessible by small bridges. On the island was a small pavilion with its own miniature garden and rooms. The Canopus, laid out in a natural valley which was further excavated to give the necessary proportions, celebrated Hadrian's visit to the original canal of the same name at Alexandria, dedicated to Serapis. The canal was decorated around one curving end and along both sides by an open Corinthian colonnade, beneath which stood statues and more obvious reminders of Egypt, such as carved crocodiles. At the far end was the semicircular *triclinium*; this was built as an apse over which ran cascades of water.

In the mountainous plateau which formed the central area of the great Persian empire, water was a priceless commodity. It controlled the evolution of the Persian garden from the establishment of the empire in the mid sixth century BC by Cyrus the Great and, despite subsequent subjection by invaders such as Alexander the Great and the Romans, Persian gardens developed the forms which inspired the Islamic garden during the seventh century AD. Cyrus was not only a successful soldier but also an enlightened ruler and in 546 BC established his capital at Pasargadae. There he built a magnificent palace around which the gardens were of integral importance.

Possibly most significant for future gardens, Cyrus's watercourses determined the complete garden plan; they were designed not only for practical irrigation purposes but also as a decorative means of establishing the gardens' essential symmetry. Plants were watered through a system of more basic open channels, often of considerable extent, to form the most important features of water distribution developed by the Persians. The underground channels were called *qanats* and were used as a means of distributing water without the evaporation to which surface channels are subject. *Qanats* were built by digging a shaft down to the water table and then excavating a tunnel – gently sloping from source to destination – to wherever the water supply was required. Some *qanats*, which can still be found in use today, ran for miles and served whole communities for cultivation and domestic use.

Just over a century after the death of Cyrus the Great one of his descendants, Cyrus the Younger, was credited with giving his garden the name which ever since has had an all-pervasive significance – paradise.

The garden was recorded by the Greek, Xenophon, who fought as one of an army of Greek mercenaries, known as the Ten Thousand, for Cyrus in his unsuccessful rebellion. Xenophon wrote that Cyrus called his garden a 'Pairidaeza', combining the two Persian words for 'around' and 'wall'. The myth of paradise represented as a garden was, of course, far older, but here for the first time was a practical link with garden design.

This duality of the spiritual and physical reflected the deep concerns of Persian life and does much to explain the strong continuity of garden development over many centuries. Gardens were for relaxation and the provision of aesthetic pleasure and the presence of water was essential; not only did it serve a basic architectural role in outlining and dividing the area of the garden, it also symbolized the presence of life, in contrast to the mountainous or desert countryside which surrounded Persian towns and villages. In addition to narrow watercourses, storage tanks, often positioned centrally in the garden, became important features combining the practical role of reservoirs with the symbolic representation of plenty; their motionless surfaces also served to reflect decorative architectural features.

Nothing more fully expressed the Persians' love of gardens and their importance as havens of beauty and peace than the tradition of weaving carpets depicting a garden layout in great detail; these enlivened the cold stone floors of palaces and houses and provided a reminder of gardens through the winter months. The most famous – and probably the largest – was the legendary 'Winter Carpet' or 'Spring of Khosru' (also called 'Chosroes' or 'Khusrau'), named after the last ruler of Persia before the Arab invasion, which covered the floor of the enormous audience hall in his palace at Ctesiphon. In this and all other similar Persian carpets which continued to be made for over a thousand years, the pattern is invariably made up around a series of water channels leading to a central water tank and enlivened with fish and waterfowl.

The central importance of gardens to Persian culture had been steadily evolving for over a thousand years when the Islamic Arabs overran the empire in 637 AD. Traditionally nomads were kept on the move by the constant search for water in the Arabian deserts and, journeying from one oasis to another, they did not have the integrated and advanced culture that came with long-established settlement. Many strands of Persian culture, not least their garden design with its emphasis on the importance and celebration of water, struck an immediate chord with the Arabs and after the achievement of supremacy the warring religious fanaticism of Islam was subdued into what became an

This section of a seventeenth-century Persian 'Winter Carpet' clearly represents the layout of a garden, divided by four main water channels centred on a rectangular water cistern.

At the Madrassa Mader-i-Shah, Isfahan (above) and Hadrian's villa, Tivoli (opposite) the motionless surface of water provides an extra dimension by reflecting surrounding architectural features and statuary.

immensely rich civilization. Within two decades of the Arab invasion of Persia the teachings of the prophet Mohammed were enshrined in the text of *The Koran*, with regular references to gardens, and most significantly to the concept of paradise as a garden, in which plentiful water fed in by the rivers of life and bubbling out of fountains was the key element. What the Arabs saw in Persian gardens matched the descriptions in the holy text of *The Koran* and the two sources of inspiration fused together to dictate the development of the Islamic garden for nearly a thousand years, notably within the area of the old Persian empire itself, and in the two opposite extremes of an expanded Islam: Moorish Spain in the west and Mughal India in the east.

After the initial Islamic subjection and the subsequent advances and retreats of invaders, Persia waited for centuries until its most spectacular flowering of gardens, the creation of the garden city at Isfahan by Abbas the Great, the Safavid ruler who lived from 1557 to 1629. Isfahan was a brilliant example of town-planning around the traditional Persian formal water garden. The backbone was the Chahar-Bagh Avenue, stretching for a mile right through the city from the bridge over the river. Along the centre of the avenue flowed a continuous canal which widened out at intervals into octagonal and square pools with fountains. From this central waterway other channels and irrigation pipes fed off on both sides. The major buildings and palaces of the town were planned around a succession of gardens, each dominated by a major water feature such as the rectangular pool which survives to reflect the teak-columned portico of the Chehel Sutun or Hall of Forty Columns. Inevitably Isfahan has witnessed considerable alteration during the ensuing centuries and the all-important central canal of the Chahar-Bagh Avenue has long ceased to flow. Nonetheless, many later buildings continued to incorporate water features and garden courtyards and thereby perpetuated the centuries-old Persian tradition that briefly re-emerged during the reign of Abbas.

The Islamic Water Garden

2

FROM THE CONQUEST OF PERSIA and the Middle East, Islam spread relentlessly through Egypt and along the seaboard of North Africa until, early in the eighth century, it made what proved to be one of its most decisive cultural steps, when the Moors crossed the Straits of Gibraltar and established a foothold in southern Spain.

Although neither as harsh or fiercely arid as the conditions in the Islamic heartland of Persia, the sub-tropical climate and terrain of Andalusia were such that water was similarly at a premium. The Moors reintroduced high-level hydraulics and irrigation systems, which had completely disappeared with the departure of the Romans. Along the valley of the Guadalquivir, where both Cordoba and Seville were built, the natural supply of water was diverted into large cisterns and reservoirs to feed vineyards planted on terraces and other crops which sustained much of the flourishing Moorish economy. The local population was steadily integrated into the way of life and culture, but the great majority of craftsmen were imported from other countries of the Islamic empire and thus continuity in architectural and garden styles was to a large extent guaranteed.

Even in the earliest examples of Moorish gardens, of which virtually nothing remains, there was evidence of a quite individual sophistication built upon the harmonious relationship of water and decorative architecture within an often complex arrangement of enclosed courtyard spaces. Indeed, it was the combination of enclosed spaces with glimpses of the surroundings and, in many cases, distant views through exquisitely decorated arcades which was one of the most successful aspects of the gardens.

Within the courtyards or patios the distribution of water was in every case the dominant feature. In fact, compared to the situation for most other Islamic gardens, the supply of water for Moorish gardens was luxuriously plentiful and this makes the intricacy of the channels and the reticence of undisturbed pools and low bubble-fountains more strikingly subtle and understated.

The Moorish Garden

In the Moorish garden of the Patio de los Naranjos, Cordoba (opposite) water is both practical, providing irrigation for the orange trees which give the court its name, and at the same time decorative.

These four views of the Generalife garden, Granada, including the Court of the Canal (opposite) and the New Gardens (overleaf), illustrate how its interlinking areas were planned around narrow canals, pools and fountains, making water the garden's single most important feature.

The great quality in the use of water in Moorish gardens – most obviously when compared with the unfettered exuberance of Renaissance gardens that followed – is the manner in which restraint is balanced with a feeling of plenty. This, more than any other feature of the gardens, gives an insight into the spirit behind their creation. No garden was ever primarily for display; rather it was a place for the celebration of natural abundance with the ever-present sight and sound of water and the luxury of deep-green foliage and the colour and scent of favoured plants such as oleanders and roses. But equally important, it was a place of privacy and contemplation, in which feelings of peaceful contentment could be evoked.

The great majority of the Moorish gardens that survive have been altered or added to in varying degrees, whether with new and more elaborate fountain jets or richer planting. But such was the simple strength and harmony of the original designs that they are still as impressive today as they must have been when originally created five or six centuries ago. One of the oldest to survive, the Patio de los Naranjos (Courtyard of the Orange Trees) in Cordoba, was created in 976 AD as an open courtyard garden beside the mosque and within the same rectangular walled enclosure. Today, the sense of connection between mosque and patio – and the contrast between dark enclosure and light openness – is diminished by dividing walls that fill in much of the original arcades, but the patio can still be seen as a prototype of much of the water garden design that followed. Within the rectangular courtyard three fountain basins overflow into a series of narrow geometrical water channels among the trees.

The Generalife at Granada, or rather on the hills of the Cerro del Sol overlooking the city, was built in the thirteenth century as a summer residence for the ruling dynasty. Taken from the original Arabic, the name means literally 'the garden of the architect' and the whole design hinges upon the successive areas of garden. Throughout, the atmosphere is one of relaxation and intimacy, brought about in part by the use of water.

The centre-piece of the garden is the Court of the Canal, where water effects the desired harmony between the small-scale design and the rich detail of architecture and planting. The long, narrow central canal runs between close planting to three-storeyed pavilions at either end, with arcaded loggias at ground level providing cool shade and underlining this effect with lotus-shaped basins whose low bubble fountains cause the water to constantly brim over; these are at either end of the canal, but

*While the use of water at the Generalife enhances the garden's atmosphere of intimacy, at the nearby Alhambra Palace the pools and fountains of the various courtyards add a delicate note to the ancient fortress's atmosphere of majestic security (*above, right *and* opposite*).*

separated from its contrastingly placid surface. The picture is completed by the rows of single jets – added after the initial garden's original creation – which arch across the canal along its full length. The almost sensual effect of such a garden, where light, shade and water in motion and repose alternate within a confined space, is a clear evocation of the Islamic paradise garden ideal, made doubly effective by the contrast with the spectacular views over the rugged hills from the mirador at one end.

The Court of the Canal is enclosed along one side by an open arcade leading to a small mosque. On terraces above the range of buildings along the other side are later gardens added in the early fourteenth century: the Patio del los Cipréses, a small secluded patio exclusively for the ladies of the Sultan's harem, and above here the Camino de los Cascades, or water stairway, the only example of one surviving in a Moorish garden. The former is completely dominated by water, a U-shaped canal filling three sides of the small enclosure and giving the impression that the central area is a miniature island, where there is a square pool into which water constantly tumbles from a raised fountain basin, on either side of which are neatly hedged oleanders. From this courtyard there is the ceaseless beckoning of the sound of water, as it descends along the channels carved into the balustrades of the water stairway and from the low fountains playing into circular pools at the foot of each flight of steps.

The Generalife was a villa, a place of undisturbed pleasure and relaxation, moods that could not be more different to the austere splendour of the Alhambra or 'Red Castle', built first and foremost as a fortress, an impenetrable hillside bastion, which indeed it proved to be, surviving as the last Moorish stronghold in the face of the advancing Christian kingdom. The construction of the Alhambra was begun in the mid thirteenth century by Mohammad ben Al-Ahmar. The creation of this secure stronghold and habitable residence focused upon the engineering feat of raising water up to the hillside site from the river Darro which flowed down from the Sierra Nevada. Although parts of the original building disappeared and were replaced by the sixteenth-century palace built by Charles V and other areas have been inevitably altered, the Islamic arrangement of a majestic series of integrated but not wholly symmetrical courtyards is still overpowering.

This is the mood reflected in the main gardens and in particular in the two most important garden courtyards, the Court of the Myrtles (also known as the Court of the Pool) and the Court of the Lions. Created by successive rulers in the mid and late fourteenth century, the two courts

In the Court of the Lions at the Alhambra the formal simplicity of the water features contrasts with and softens the powerful effect of the surrounding architecture.

represent one of the sublime contrasts in the spatial use of water in gardens, in the one expansive and reposeful, in the other closely limited in area and yet vigorous. The central rectangular tank of the Court of the Myrtles, flanked by closely clipped myrtle hedges outside paved paths along both sides, has nothing to detract from the serene effect of its broad surface, reflecting the open arcades at either end whose slender columns support a screen of decorated plasterwork. The pool's rectangular symmetry is only broken in the simplest possible fashion by the small ground-level circular fountain basins and short channels that feed water in at either end.

The breathtaking simplicity of the Court of the Myrtles is enhanced by the transition to the Court of the Lions, adjacent to the south-east, where clusters of alabaster columns supporting highly decorated arcades around all sides create a lively interplay of light and shade. In the most traditional of all Islamic patterns, the court is divided into a quatrefoil by narrow rills fed by bubble fountains in small sunken circular basins and joining at a hexagonal pool in whose centre twelve monumental carved lions support a twelve-sided fountain basin. The visual impact of the court derives from the simplicity of the composition of water and architecture juxtaposed with the richness of decoration. At the same time, the arrangement of water, the cross of minimal channels which link the open court and shaded arcades, focusing on the fountain centre-piece, demonstrate a level of sophistication seen elsewhere in the Alhambra in the Court of the Cuarto Dorado – the preliminary to the Court of the Myrtles after the three main entrance courts – where the centre-piece is a low circular basin overflowing into an octagonal pool.

After the final ousting of the Moors when their artistic influence was perpetuated in Christian Spain it was often most evident in the arrangement of gardens in the Mudejar style. The garden of the Alcazar Palace in Seville, rebuilt in the fourteenth century after the city had been captured by the Christians, is the largest surviving example and its various courtyards, although perhaps lacking the subtle continuity between enclosure and open space found at the Generalife for instance, perpetuate the tradition in their central low fountain basins set in paving and reflecting the pattern of coloured tiles. Perhaps most important, the quality of Moorish gardens ensured that future Spanish gardens would adopt the concept of a courtyard enlivened by the sight and sound of water as a constantly recurring theme.

These miniatures show Babur, the first Mughal emperor, organizing the creation of his favourite garden, Bagh-i-Wafa, the Garden of Fidelity. The location of the garden is unknown, but may have been in the region of Kabul.

The Mughal Garden

Far removed from the Moorish gardens were the creations of the Mughal emperors in northern India. Yet the same essential aspirations which inspired all Islamic gardens are immediately evident. Descended from Genghis Khan and Tamerlane, whose conquering armies swept out of central Asia in the thirteenth and fourteenth centuries, the Mughals gained effective control of northern India under Babur after his defeat of the Sultan of Delhi in 1526. Babur subsequently established his capital at Agra and it is from this date that the artistic flowering of the Mughal empire began, to be continued through five successive generations of rulers until the death of Shah Jahan in 1658. While Babur's son Humayun spent most of his reign in enforced exile from India and his son Akbar was primarily preoccupied with the military and administrative integration of the empire, the last two generations, Akbar's son Jahangir and Shah Jahan created the majority of the great Mughal gardens that survive to give the dynasty its fabulous reputation as garden makers.

The Mughals reproduced the rectangular paradise garden of Persia, the *chahar-bagh*; yet, notably in the tomb gardens of Babur's successors and in the lakeside gardens of Kashmir, they radically transformed it in both scale and concept. They also elevated the already central role of water in the gardens to become the controlling factor both in terms of a

garden's design and its whole atmosphere. The site at Agra was chosen because of its proximity to the river Jumna and one of the most symbolic features of all the Mughal gardens laid out at Agra, Delhi or anywhere else along the river, was the immediate juxtaposition of the formalized water in the garden and the ever-present river flowing past. Initially, the first gardens created by Babur were dependent upon wells for their water, but it was not long before a system of canals was created to bring water directly from the river, thereby greatly increasing both the quantity available and the natural gravity pressure.

Part of the structure of Ram Bagh, one of the three gardens that Babur made in Agra on the opposite bank of the Jumna from his fort, survives to show that the garden was fed by a large well and divided geometrically by water channels. It was here that his body was temporarily interred before being moved to a burial ground at Kabul, his original home.

The first of the true tomb gardens laid out by the Mughals to survive – although without any water – is that of Babur's son Humayun, built at Delhi by his wife Haji Begum during her husband's enforced exile from India and completed in 1573 six years after his death. It shows all the characteristics and qualities which were to be steadily refined by his successors, a harmony of symbolism and ordered physical beauty on a scale previously unknown in Islamic gardens. The tomb, built of red sandstone and decorated with white marble, is set in the centre of a walled-in square of some thirty acres, the focal point of a *chahar-bagh* and of the four main watercourses.

The sub-division of the area was dictated by symbols of great importance to the Mughals, in particular the number eight and the octagon which represented a fusion of the square and the circle. Thirty-two square plots are divided by narrow watercourses with square limestone pools at their junctions. At the corners of the main walk enclosing the tomb the sunken water channels flow into octagonal pools. The supply of water came directly from the Jumna into a long rectangular tank hidden along one outside wall. This storage tank enabled sufficient pressure to be built up to guarantee a flow along all the water channels and into narrow underground irrigation pipes which fed off to each plot, before the water was released to flow into the garden beneath one of four axial gateways and over a *chadar* or sloping water-chute, which became one of the most innovative features in Mughal gardens.

Each of Humayun's successors built his own tomb garden, but

without doubt the supreme example was the Taj Mahal, built by the emperor Shah Jahan in memory of his favourite wife Mumtaz Mahal, a Persian princess and the niece of Jahangir's wife. She died in 1631 only three years after Shah Jahan became emperor and work on the tomb and its garden began in 1632, to be completed in 1654. The exquisite architecture of the white marble building notwithstanding, the most radical element of the Taj Mahal was its position, not central in the *chahar-bagh* as had become the Mughal tradition, but raised up on a platform at one end overlooking the Jumna on its other side, symbolically suspended between the orderly human world on one side and naturally flowing eternity on the other. Instead, the centre of the square garden was filled with a square pool reflecting the whole façade of the tomb. It is interesting to consider the completed Taj Mahal in the contemporary European context for, in 1656, two years after its completion, André Le Nôtre began work on Vaux-le-Vicomte, where the garden contained a similar central pool designed to reflect the château's whole façade.

At Shalamar Bagh, Kashmir, a raised stone platform, surrounded by water, originally supported the throne of the emperor Akbar.

Water makes an interesting pattern as it flows down a chadar *at Nishat Bagh, Kashmir.*

Around the central pool the Taj Mahal garden was laid out in exemplary Mughal style, the four main canals leading to the centre and the main squares sub-divided into smaller plots in multiples of eight by a grid of water channels. On the four corners of the garden and at either end of the riverside terrace were octagonal pavilions. Although Shah Jahan was confined to only seeing his wife's tomb from a cell in the Agra Fort, across a sweeping bend in the Jumna, where he was imprisoned by his son for the last few years of his life, the enduring vision of the Taj Mahal is of its pristine white dome and flanking pavilions and minarets shimmering on the surface of the garden's great central pool and rippling across the garden's network of canals.

In 1586 the emperor Akbar took control of Kashmir and opened the way for the development of arguably the richest vein of Mughal gardens, where abundant water was celebrated in a manner which went beyond the conventional garden boundaries to make design links with the surrounding landscape. The climate of the region at the foot of the Himalayas provided relief from the annually oppressive conditions on the north Indian plains. Close to the capital at Srinagar and focusing on Lake Dal in the Vale of Kashmir, many hundreds of Mughal gardens were created during the reigns of Jahangir and Shah Jahan. The gardens made maximum use of the water coming off the mountains into the lake and, in their siting alone which was guided by a desire to maximize the effect of the mountains on one side and the waters of the lake on the other, they represented landscape design of almost unparalleled greatness.

The central theme of these gardens was the control and distribution of descending water, different from the centuries-old Islamic tradition of formalized water features dictating a design within an enclosed space, and yet still inspired by the same basic principle of a rectangle sub-divided by water features. As contemporary accounts and a number of the surviving gardens demonstrate, in Kashmir the volume of water available and the descending levels of the gardens allowed for spectacular variety. Traditional canals and pools were constantly shrouded in the spray from hosts of fountain jets, all gravity fed; a change in level between terraces allowed the water to cascade over broad falls or to fall more decoratively over the often richly carved surfaces of marble *chenars* or water-chutes, so angled as to benefit from the maximum play of light. In some gardens the water descended without break along sloping channels. If exhilarating and full of vitality, the gardens were also imbued with an air of serenity by the limitless grandeur of their surroundings and by the privacy within individual terraces.

The most renowned of the Lake Dal gardens to survive is Shalamar Bagh, begun by Jahangir and his wife Nur Jahan and continued by his son Shah Jahan. The garden is on three descending levels and was designed to be approached by boat from Lake Dal via a long canal. As well as its fabled reputation suggested by the name 'place of love', it has been constantly admired for the combination of its perfect symmetry and architectural detail. The garden rises along a central canal, with each of the succession of squares on either side subdivided by waterways. The garden's pavilions were built either completely surrounded by water or spanning the central canal and in one, which has disappeared, Jahangir gave audiences sitting on a black marble throne set over a waterfall. On the uppermost level of the garden, called the *zenata* and used only by the ladies of the court, Shah Jahan built the surviving black marble pavilion, completely enclosed and seemingly marooned by water.

The other main garden to survive beside the lake is Nishat Bagh, created by Nur Jahan's brother. In area it is larger than Shalamar, rising through twelve terraces, but its design follows a similar pattern when approached by boat from the lake, focusing upon a broad central canal which descends from terrace to terrace down broad *chadars* to flow through rectangular pools studded with fountain jets.

Of all the Mughal emperors, Jahangir was the one most fond of Kashmir and his reign revolved around the annual progressions northwards from Agra to Lahore and on to Strinagar. Two of his favourite gardens, Achabal and Vernag, were created away from Lake Dal at the foot of the mountains that border the lower corner of the Vale of Kashmir. Both are fed by gushing natural springs; at Achabal, in particular, the original design of the garden around the powerful flow is still quite evident as the water descends from the huge cascade at the top along a central canal. This canal broadens into square pools and the water flows beneath the garden's pavilions or rushes unhindered down two *chenars* descending the length of the garden on either side.

At Vernag nothing remains of Jahangir's pavilions or other architectural features, but the water which issues from a spring of centuries-old religious significance for Kashmiris still flows into a large octagonal pool surrounded by twenty-four arched recesses and thence via a descending canal of some three hundred yards to the Bihat river. Jahangir died in 1627 on the return journey south from Kashmir, which he constantly referred to as paradise; he wished to be buried in his garden at Vernag, but his wife interred his body in the garden of Shahdara at Lahore.

The seemingly endless vista of a canal stretches up towards the mountains beyond at Nishat Bagh.

Shalamar Bagh (left), Nishat Bagh (below) and Vernag (below left) demonstrate how the Mughal emperors adapted the water features of the traditional Persian garden to the landscape of Kashmir.

Whether along the river Jumna at Agra and Delhi, in the Himalayan foothills of Kashmir, or in the other major centres of their empire, such as Lahore, the Mughals laid out gardens which saw the treatment of water achieve new heights of ingenuity. The physical and symbolic dominance of the design and the quality of individual features are remarkable. Inextricably linked to the superlative architecture which they were intended to complement, the gardens also retained a vital bond with features of the surrounding natural landscape. Within each garden the variation of mood was dictated by changes in the treatment of water, with a rarely equalled harmony of movement and contrasting stillness, resulting in a complex interplay of sound, light and shade and reflection.

The flow of water through pavilions and along a central course at Achabal is one of the most impressive features of any Mughal garden.

Water Features *from the Islamic to the Italian Garden*

3

DESPITE a long chronological overlap, the move from Islam to Renaissance Italy marks a vast cultural shift and the use of water in the garden undergoes a transition. From being primarily representative and symbolic – the soul of a garden, and therefore often deployed with great subtlety – it becomes first and foremost ornamental, a means of expression and the opportunity to impress by combining decoration with movement. The Renaissance mood of artistic and intellectual confidence and vigour, the strong sense of release from the confinement of the Dark and Middle Ages and the reaffirmation of man's central position in the natural and cosmic orders were celebrated by water in motion, initially in the fountain, being the perfect medium in which to fuse living, physical and ornamental elements. Subsequently, the spectacular and yet totally controlled displays of water in High Renaissance and Baroque gardens emphasized the degree of human superiority in the natural order.

The evolution of the early Renaissance gardens from the cautious enclosure of the medieval *hortus conclusus* to the pleasure garden of a villa can be seen substantially in terms of the expansion of the role of water. In addition, intellectual admiration for the ancients, combined with the increasingly tangible knowledge provided by archaeology, enabled gardeners to develop a style that both emulated the achievement of their admired Greek and Roman predecessors and provided an ideal outlet for rapidly developing artistic, architectural and engineering skills. Petrarch wrote with admiration of the inspiration that led men to 'erect altars at places where great streams burst suddenly from hidden sources', while the later Roman humanist, Angelo Colocci, consciously evoked the world of ancient Rome with the figure of a water nymph lying in the arch of an aqueduct in his short-lived garden. As the Renaissance garden became more architecturally diverse and confident, so these developments were reflected in the treatment of water, which became increasingly by integral to the gardens' composition as well as being the most exhilarating decorative feature.

The Villa Garzoni, Collodi, incorporates a large number of ingenious and amusing water features in its design, such as this droll figure of a water carrier.

The River Gods, a sculpture and water feature, forms a dramatic end piece to the water chain at the Villa Farnese, Caprarola (opposite).

The cascade at Wilhelmshöhe.

Cascade

One of the most exhilarating of water features, the cascade, appears in a number of variations, such as the *catena d'acqua* and water staircase; they were especially prevalent in Italian Renaissance gardens. They were also created as formal architectural features in classical gardens and as naturalistic features in the landscape gardens of the eighteenth century and later. The cascade is an essentially European feature, although examples can be also be found in some of the Mughal gardens in Kashmir. Some of the most ornate cascades were built in French classical gardens, such as Saint-Cloud, but elsewhere in Europe individual examples were either larger, as in the examples at Wilhelmshöhe and the Palazzo Reale, Caserta, or more sumptuous as at La Granja and Peterhof. The only formal cascade in England is at Chatsworth, but a number were built in eighteenth-century landscapes at the point where water flowed into a lake, as in the example in Capability Brown's park at Bowood which was designed by Charles Hamilton. Far from being an architectural, symmetrical descent of water, these examples were often highly picturesque rockeries.

Catena d'Acqua

The *catena d'acqua* (literally 'chain of water') was a variation of the cascade developed and perfected during the Italian Renaissance. Water was channelled down the centre of an architectural ramp, contained on either side by stone carved into a scroll pattern to give the chain-like appearance. The two most celebrated examples are at the Villa Lante and the Casino garden of the Palazzo Farnese, Caprarola. In the former the stonework containing the water is carved into crayfish, the emblem of the owner, Cardinal Gambara.

A catena d'acqua, *water chain, at the Villa Lante.*

Chadar

A type of narrow, sloping water chute peculiar to Islamic gardens and perfected in the Mughal gardens of Kashmir. The stone channels were used to carry water through the descent from one terrace to another – often along the garden's perimeters rather than in a central cascade – and were angled so as to reflect sunlight to the maximum possible degree.

The chadar *at Nishat Bagh, Kashmir.*

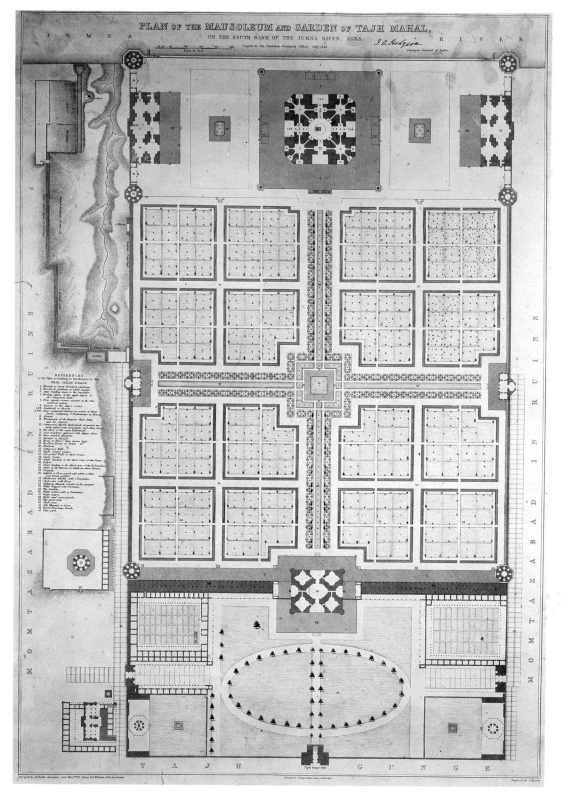

This plan of the Taj Mahal, dating from 1828, clearly shows the chahar-bagh *form of division into four by water channels.*

Chahar-Bagh

The quatrefoil foundation of all Islamic gardens, in which the square or rectangular garden area is divided equally by cruciform water channels. The name was adapted to some individual sites such as Chahar-Bagh Avenue in Isfahan, the central axis of the town along which flowed a canal.

Chute

Unlike cascades, water chutes allow water to flow downwards without a break. They are often used in steep or terraced gardens as an ornamental means of carrying water from one level to another, as in the *chadars* of the Mughal gardens.

Fountain

The most important architectural and engineering water feature in gardens, Eastern and Western, is almost certainly the fountain. No other features has attained such variety in both its decorative and technological aspects. Throughout history – at least until the contemporary period – the most successful and impressive fountains have been supplied by water powered by gravity, rather than by any artificial means such as steam power and, with a guaranteed water source at regular pressure, the most complicated element has normally been a system of supply pipes of decreasing size and of valves and stopcocks to control and distribute the water throughout an often complex array of fountain jets, whether within one basin or distributed throughout a whole garden.

Fountains can be divided into two categories, those decorated with sculpture and those without, where the play of water in itself is the primary attraction. Of the former, the fountains of Renaissance Italian gardens achieved a peak of artistic quality in their sculptures, produced by the leading artists of the time, although even they were eclipsed in scale and splendour by the fountains that later adorned the gardens of Versailles. In the primarily architectural gardens which predominated in Renaissance and Baroque Europe and which have continued to be made ever since, decorative fountain basins have been an integral part of garden design. They have provided the focal points for vistas and axes and, in many cases and notably at Versailles, they have been one of the main means of illustrating a garden's complicated iconography. The wearing away of the material of a fountain by constantly moving water has led to a preference for marble or metals rather than types of stone.

Where sculpture is not incorporated, a fountain has had to rely on the height of its jet to achieve its effect, as in the case of the Emperor fountain at Chatsworth. In Islamic gardens, where figurative sculpture is banned by the text of *The Koran*, fountains have often been refreshingly simple, emphasizing their primary purpose of providing a sense of cool relief from oppressively hot surroundings. One of the most characteristic styles was the bubble fountain, in which water was forced

A design for a fountain at Hatfield House, Hertfordshire, by Salomon de Caus (1612).

up just enough to break the surface of a pool or basin and force the water to constantly overflow.

In the contemporary garden, fountains have proved the ideal medium for introducing modern abstract sculpture into the garden, as well as developing into some of the most spectacular features of landscape architecture. The vibrancy and potential excitement of water in motion has remained unchanged throughout the centuries, providing the backcloth for constantly changing styles of sculptural or architectural decoration. The electric pump has become widely adopted as the means of providing water for a fountain jet.

Fountain at the Casa de Pilatos, Seville.

Giochi d'Acqua

The Italian phrase *giochi d'acqua*, literally meaning 'water games', were often played at the expense of unsuspecting visitors who were soaked by a jet or spray of water suddenly appearing from a concealed site, such as a wall beside a path or the seat of a bench. The phrase was also used to include water-powered automata, which achieved a peak of ingenuity in the Renaissance garden. Such features were described in Latin texts, but they really came to the fore in Renaissance and Baroque gardens throughout Europe, when such jokes greatly appealed to the contemporary sense of humour and when the technical achievements of automata, such as birds that were made to sing or figures made to move by water power, were greatly admired. For this reason the garden of Pratolino was among the most admired in Europe. *Giochi d'acqua* were frequently incorporated into grottoes.

A water joke in the form of a tree at Chatsworth, Derbyshire.

Various fountain forms at the Generalife (above left), Warwick Castle (below left) and Kleve (above).

Grotto

In ancient Greece springs which emerged from hillside caves often became sacred sites, reputed to be the haunts of gods, nymphs and other legendary figures. From this beginning, the grotto took on a symbolic significance and came to be especially admired as a garden feature, endowed with strong classical connotations and capable of extraordinary effects. The crude original of a damp hillside cave with rough, stony walls constantly dripping water, was to be reproduced in European gardens for centuries, often embellished to a fantastic degree. From rough dwellings they became places of pure fantasy: vaulted ceilings studded with crystal stalactites, rough walls hewn into monumental sculptures, carvings of weird animals set in niches and invariably water in some form or other, whether spurting from concealed jets to soak visitors, powering automata or gushing into a pool from a spring-like source.

The great majority of Italian Renaissance gardens had a grotto, usually celebrating a specific iconographical programme at the same time as providing the opportunity for Renaissance ingenuity to demonstrate its full extent. In European societies which greatly enjoyed display and which were fascinated by the suggestion of either the grotesque or the supernatural, the appeal of grottoes in gardens which told a story as well as presenting visual delights survived throughout Europe well into the nineteenth century. Spectacular examples were incorporated into French classical gardens, German gardens and into eighteenth-century English landscapes.

The Grotte d'Orphée, designed by Thomas Francini, at Saint-Germain-en-Laye.

The magnificent grotto in the Boboli Gardens, Florence.

A wall mask serving as a spout at the Villa Reale, Castello.

Mascaron

The *mascaron* (wall mask) is a small decorative feature, sometimes purely architectural, as when decorating the keystone of an arch or doorway, but incorporating water when adorning fountains, cascades, or walls, when the grotesque face spouts water from its mouth. Popular in Mannerist gardens and in many European gardens of the seventeenth and eighteenth centuries, the *mascaron* is potentially a most useful means of introducing water into the small contemporary garden, when mounted on a wall and spouting water into a basin or a dipping-well.

A nappe at Wroxton Abbey, Oxfordshire.

Nappe

A *nappe* is a sheet of water falling over a dam or weir, or over a formally stepped cascade of the kind created to great effect in many of the Mughal gardens in Kashmir.

Nymphaeum

Nymphaea were incorporated into gardens from the times of ancient Greece and Rome as architectural representations or celebrations of their mythological inhabitants. Whether designed as rooms, set into a terrace or free-standing in the form of a screen, the traditional model is generally highly decorative with columns, statuary and other architectural devices and a central recess or apse which contains a source of water.

The nymphaeum of the Villa di Papa Giulia, Rome.

Spout

The spout is an alternative to the fountain jet, where water is poured rather than forced out under pressure. Water emerged from such spouts in many of the earliest, simple fountains, in the gardens of Egypt and Mesopotamia, for instance. In gardens all over the world water has been channelled into decorative spouts then fed into pools or canals, as in the dolphins' heads at Courances whose mouths spout water into one of the main pools.

Spouts in the form of both real and fabulous creatures: Klein-Grienicke (above left), Courances (left) and the Villa Reale (above).

The water staircase at Holker Hall, Cumbria.

Water Staircase

The water staircase is a variation of the cascade in which the descent of water is formalized over steps. Such features were ideally suited to the descending layout of many Italian gardens, notably the Villa Aldobrandini and the Villa Garzoni, while some of the most impressive water staircases were built in French classical gardens such as Sceaux; one of the best examples is the restored *rivière* at the château of Villette.

Water Theatre

Architectural theatres were popular features in Italian Renaissance gardens, the best known examples surviving at the Villa Marlia and Isola Bella. At the Villa Aldobrandini water was introduced to spectacular effect in the water theatre built into the curving retaining wall of the garden's main terrace. The whole wall is richly decorated; arched niches contain statues behind water jets, and there is a central figure of Atlas with water pouring from the base of his globe and from a fountain on the retaining wall above.

The figure of Atlas dominates the water theatre at the Villa Aldobrandini, Frascati (opposite).

The Italian Style

4

A CLEAR PROGRESSION in the use of water can be observed from the sculpted fountain pieces, the nymphaea and grottoes of early Renaissance gardens, which were individual features within a garden, to the Baroque exuberance of the Villa Garzoni. Bramante's plan for the Vatican's Cortile del Belvedere, commissioned by Pope Julius II and begun in 1503, transformed garden design by its treatment of a sloping site with terraces linked by ramped stairways flanking a strong central axis, thereby adding visual drama to perspective. In no area was his influence more dramatic than in the use of water. Thereafter, in the sloping, often dramatic, sites so favoured by Italians, water was employed to give a central theme of movement through a garden, a sense of progression with a finite starting-point and an eventual place of rest. Once this principle had been established, it could be adapted in limitless ways to test both the engineering and architectural skills of garden makers, and as water emerged from natural *bosci* at a garden's highest point and thence steadily descended, so it became representative and symbolic, journeying through a garden and bringing life in a host of different guises.

The decorative quality of the water features of early Renaissance gardens was immediately evident in one of the first Medici gardens, the Villa Careggi, where the rectangular garden's central fountain was crowned with Verrocchio's bronze figure, 'Boy with a Dolphin'. It was more extensively emphasized in the garden of the later Medici villa, at Castello, designed from 1540 for Cosimo I, first by Niccolo Tribolo and, after Tribolo's premature death in 1550, by Bartolomeo Ammanati and Bernardo Buontalenti.

It was the water features, the fountains, statuary and the grotto, which expressed the Renaissance spirit of the garden. The centre-piece was a secluded pool from which arose an elaborately carved fountain by Tribolo surmounted by Giambologna's bronze statue of Venus wringing out her wet hair and representing Florence rising from the water. Closer to the villa, but still on the garden's central axis, was a second fountain with an equally impressive sculpture of Hercules wrestling with Antaeus by Ammanati. Here an important development was made in

At the Villa Medici, Castello, Florence, the monumental figure of January by Ammanati crouches on a small island in a pool of water on the garden's upper terrace.

Water appears with a flourish in the garden of Villa Garzoni, Collodi, spouting from the trumpet of the figure of Fame into the garden's upper pool and introducing its strong, vigorous Baroque character (opposite).

At the Villa Medici, Castello (above) it was the water features of the garden, notably the great fountains, which gave this fifteenth-century garden its Renaissance vitality. Water was also an essential part of the design of another great garden of the Medici, the Boboli Gardens (below).

that, as well as the spouts of water issuing from the various levels of the decorated fountain base, the sculpture was given vivid animation by the powerful jet of water issuing from the mouth of Antaeus. Much of the garden's original character has been lost since the removal of the Venus fountain in the late eighteenth century and the repositioning of the Hercules fountain in the central position, but without the encircling cypress trees.

Fortunately, however, the major features at the top of the garden still survive, including the monumental bronze figure of January (sometimes called the Apennines) by Ammanati, which crouches shivering and dripping in the centre of a pool, and the grotto dug into the slope immediately beneath. The water issued into the grotto from the pool above in two streams representing the Arno and Mugnone rivers. The grotto was notable for its great shell-lined niches, allegorical figures of animals such as a camel and an elephant and its *giochi d'acqua*, those surprise jets of water which would issue from the floor to drench unsuspecting visitors and which were much favoured in sixteenth-century Italian gardens. Possibly the garden's most ingenious water device, which no longer survives, was the marble table set in a holm oak tree where a fountain of water issued from a vase set on the table – a device later repeated at Pratolino.

In the Boboli Gardens of the Medici's most magnificent palace, the Pitti in the centre of Florence, Bernardo Buontalenti designed the enormous Grotto Grande in three parts towards the end of the sixteenth century. It remains the most impressive grotto of the period, with its great figures of slaves roughly carved by Michelangelo, dank passages of artificial stone and shell-encrusted fountains and, in the innermost recess, Giambologna's nude figure of Venus. Probably Buontalenti's most ingenious feature was his means of lighting the interior by means of a crystal fish bowl fixed into the circular opening of the vaulted roof.

The overall character of the Florentine Renaissance gardens and the fountains and grottoes that were their most distinctive features was established thanks to the superlative decorative skills of the craftsmen employed by the Medici family. Similar achievements were also evident in the gardens being created in and around Rome, but with the vital difference that the decorative features were incorporated into schemes that, in their own right, marked radical progress in design and in the use of water. This difference is best demonstrated by the three most celebrated Roman villa gardens of the period, the Palazzo Farnese at Caprarola, the Villa d'Este at Tivoli and the Villa Lante at Bagnaia.

Caprarola, designed for Cardinal Alessandro Farnese, was the work of Giacomo Vignola, one of the two or three most significant figures in the development of Renaissance gardens and an architect with a particular aptitude for garden design. His architectural work at Caprarola, carried out between 1556 and 1583, transformed a forbidding fortress into a monumental pentagonal *palazzo* standing above the small town of Caprarola, with spectacular views over the surrounding Cimini Hills. The scale and character of the building and of the landscape dictated that no garden plan would ever completely surround the *palazzo* itself. Instead, Vignola positioned walled enclosures opposite two adjacent sides of the pentagon, characterizing them as winter and summer gardens. His intention was to maximize the impression of the building's great size by contrast, hence his siting of the casino garden some four hundred yards beyond the summer garden at the end of a woodland path. Although the Casino garden was actually made after Vignola's death in 1573 it has always been accepted that it was his design.

It is the harmony of intimacy, scale and perfectly conceived water features which is the Casino garden's great success. From the point of arrival there is an upward progression through alternating straight axes and double curves, given unity by water features. Looking down the garden the central composition of the garden is aligned with the central three-arched loggia of the Casino building which overlooks the first level of the garden decorated with fountains: recumbent bearded river gods pour water from cornucopia into a huge urn, whence it overflows into a large arched basin before being channelled down the scalloped *catena d'acqua* in the centre of a walled ramp to a circular pool with a simple single-jet fountain in the centre at the lowest level.

Vignola achieved perfection on a small scale in Caprarola's Casino garden and a number of the features were repeated at the Villa Lante. But it was the impressive size of Farnese's palazzo which spurred on his rival Cardinal Ippolito d'Este to create what has become acknowledged as the supreme garden of the High Renaissance, the Villa d'Este, where water was used with outstanding genius. The garden's fame has caused it to be amongst the most visited and described of any in the world, but no amount of attention can diminish the effects of bravado and complexity in its conception and design. The Cardinal's clear ambition was that his garden should represent his own and his family's prestige and good taste both literally and iconographically; the antiquarian and architect Pirro Ligorio provided the designs which transformed the ambition into brilliant reality.

The theatrical catena d'acqua (above), *which Vignola conceived as the centre-piece of the Casino garden at the Palazzo Farnese, Caprarola, and one of the garden's fountains* (below), *together exemplify the vigour of the Italian treatment of water in garden design.*

The position of the villa at the top of a steep north-facing slope on one side of the town of Tivoli, with views across the plain towards Rome in one direction and towards the Sabine Hills in another, was chosen so that the garden would derive the maximum benefit from the dramatic falling away of the land. The guiding principle in the garden's creation was the passage of water from the top of the garden to the bottom through a series of individual but linked levels. Even before any of the garden's stupendous ornaments and decorations had been put into position, the underlying engineering had already set the Villa d'Este apart from most other gardens. Water was diverted from the river Anio via a conduit and a long aqueduct from the Monte Sant' Angelo some distance away, to be fed in sufficient quantity – an estimated 1,200 litres per second – into the garden where the natural descent further reinforced the effects of gravity. What Ligorio achieved for Cardinal Ippolite was a demonstration of natural power and a clear indication of man's ability to adapt and control this power and to enhance it with ornament in a manner which greatly appealed to the patrons of the Renaissance.

The garden of the Villa d'Este at Tivoli is completely dominated by water features of the utmost ingenuity, ranging from the magnificent Terrace of One Hundred Fountains (opposite) to the witty combination of statuary and water in smaller set pieces (above and left).

From the accounts of successive visitors, such as Montaigne towards the end of the sixteenth century and John Evelyn some half a century later, we know that it was the lavish, ceaseless quantity of water which most impressed them. Overall, it was the effortless symmetry of the design – the terraces descending along a central axis via ramped stairways and successive fountain basins and leading off in both directions to more water features at their ends – which enabled the succession of spectacles to have maximum effect. Among the most important were the huge Organ Fountain and the Owl Fountain, in both of which the noise of water was as important as the visual effect, the Dragon Fountain on the main central axis, the Rometta Fountain which represented the seven hills of Rome and the Terrace of One Hundred Fountains stretching across the garden, where three lines of jets of water spouted into stone troughs between stone eagles (the cardinal's crest), *fleur-de-lys*, small obelisks and carved boats, all set in front of a series of a hundred reliefs depicting scenes from Ovid's *Metamorphoses*.

Such classical convolutions were essential to the whole make-up of the garden and to the fusion of the decorative and water features. The garden is also notable for the complex arrangement and sheer quantity of smaller water features: stair-rails carved into water chutes, sphinxes spouting water from their two breasts, only to be outdone by the multi-breasted figure of Diana of Ephesus and the variety of effects produced

The Fountain of the Organ (opposite left) at the Villa d'Este; this garden has always intrigued artists and has been depicted in numerous styles: here, a seventeenth-century engraving of the Rometta fountain (opposite below) and a drawing by the eighteenth-century French artist, Hubert Robert, of the Fountain of the Oval (right).

by the fountains from great curtains of water to towering single jets or a multitude of small spouts falling into a pool.

The Villa d'Este illustrated the controlled vitality and energy of the Renaissance. Similarly dominated by water, but to quite different effect, is the Villa Lante, fortunately one of the best preserved of all Renaissance gardens and to most observers the consummate example by virtue of its spatial perfection. The garden is attributed to Vignola and, although his authorship is undocumented, it would seem to be without doubt, is strongly suggested in a letter from Cardinal Alessandro Farnese, for whom Vignola worked at Caprarola, to his relation and the patron of the Villa Lante, Cardinal Gambara, written in 1568. '... as Vignola has already been to see Your Holiness and will do whatever you command of him, there is nothing further for me to do in response to your letter.' It would appear that Vignola, also working for Gambara at Viterbo (of which Gambara was Bishop), began work on the garden almost immediately and that the major work was completed by his death in 1573.

At the Villa Lante, Bagnaia, Vignola's control of water throughout the garden was particularly ingenious and varied: The Dolphins (above left) and The Fountain of the River Gods (above). The stone boats in the water parterre (left) contain musketeers who shoot water from their muskets; the stone table (opposite) has a central trough filled with water for cooling wine.

After acquiring the Villa Lante in 1590, Cardinal Montalto stamped his personal influence on the garden by replacing the original fountain in the centre of the water parterre with a group of four youths holding aloft a star – his family's device (above top). *The Fountain of the Lights* (above) *has jets rising from stonework in the form of Roman oil lamps.*

It was the garden rather than the actual villa which was of primary importance to Cardinal Gambara. In the final plan this was confirmed by the radical feature of placing twin square casinos on either side of the garden's central axis, crucially emphasizing the spatial balance of the descending levels. These are gentle, portraying in logical fashion progress from the Golden Age of Roman literature to the subduing of nature by human art achieved in modern Renaissance civilization. Only one of the pavilions, the Palazzina Gambara, was completed in the cardinal's time; the other, the Palazzina Montalto, as its name suggests, was completed for his successor, Cardinal Montalto, by the architect Carlo Maderna. The highest point of the garden is on the edge of the *barco* or hunting part laid out earlier on the hillside above. The garden is linked to the park on the uppermost of the garden's terraces by the Fountain of the Deluge, fed by water from the park and flanked by twin pavilions representing the Houses of the Muses.

The regular appearance of Cardinal Gambara's crayfish crest throughout the garden and the replacement of the original fountain in the centre of the four pools of the lowest water terrace with one of four boys holding up his own crest of mounts and a star confirm that the Villa Lante was no different to any other Renaissance garden in celebrating the status and achievement of a patron. But most observers agree that it represents the highest achievement in the combination of the natural motion of water and architecture to present a picture which suggests more than the individual physical features of which it is composed.

If one direction for the Renaissance garden was towards the proportional perfection of the Villa Lante, another route explored the contemporary fascination with curiosities, artifice and with the darker side of nature.

Mannerism had its influence on gardens as it did in every area of Renaissance art and, in the case of the Villa Pratolino, was responsible for the greatest degree of technical ingenuity, making it probably the most renowned of the sixteenth century and referred to as 'the garden of marvels' until its sad demise in 1819, when it was replaced by a *giardino inglese*, as fashion dictated.

Created for Francesco di Medici between 1569–81, Pratolino was the work of Bernardo Buontalenti who later made the Grotto Grande in the Boboli Gardens and bore the grand title of 'director of *spettacoli* for the Medici'. At Pratolino he was able to indulge his fascination fully with water-driven mechanical devices and curiosities which represented in animated form both animals and humans in various working activities.

The villa was sited halfway down a slope with the two distinct areas of garden above and below, the unifying factor of which was the downward flow of water. Rather than the architectural control and distribution of the water, it was the complexity of Buontalenti's system of valves and stopcocks to control the gadgetry that was so remarkable.

A five-kilometre aqueduct fed water to the top of the garden where a statue of Jupiter overlooked a reservoir pool and hedged labyrinth. Below this, on the main axis, was the famous figure of Apennine by Giambologna – the only surviving feature today – whose hand presses down on the head of a fish seemingly forcing water out of its mouth; from this point in the garden an amphitheatre cut into the hillside extended to the villa. Below the villa a balustraded terrace stood over a series of grottoes and from here an avenue was cut between *bosci* with flanking stone walls from which a series of single jets sprayed out along its whole length. At the lowest level the central axis terminated in a large basin into which the water fell from a statue by Valerio Cioli of a washerwoman squeezing water out of a 'cloth' of white marble. Any apparent symmetry along the central axis was diminished by Buontalenti's random arrangement through the garden of fountains, grottoes and pools, each with its own particular identity, by the unexpected *giochi d'acqua*, such as those in the main grotto described by Montaigne, activated as the innocent visitor sat on a bench: 'By a single movement the whole grotto was filled with water, and all the seats squirt water on to your backside …'; on the steps up to the villa would suddenly appear 'a thousand jets of water from every two steps on that staircase.'

This engraving (left) by Stefano della Bella shows the central fountain walk at Pratolino. Giambologna's figure of Apennine (above) demonstrates the scale of the features in the garden; the giant's hand is pressed on the head of a monster, seemingly forcing water from its mouth.

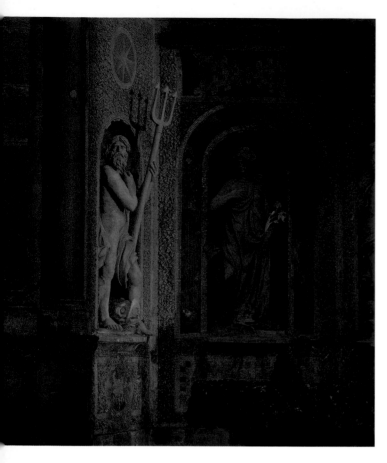

*T*he water theatre at Villa
Aldobrandini, Frascati (above *and*
opposite); *its dramatic centre-piece is a
figure of Atlas holding aloft a globe.*

Indeed, surprise was the ever-present feature of Buontalenti's creation: 'He filled toy theatres with little automata which moved in response to the movements of the water, and set them in grottoes near the villa, by the statue of Apennine and in Cupid's Grotto. Hydraulic organs were placed on Mount Parnassus and around the garden were scattered dozens of boxes containing bellows operated by water and fitted with whistles which imitated the calls of a wide variety of different species of birds.'

In the area around Rome the main centre for gardens was Frascati, revived on the site of the ancient Etruscan town of Tusculum, which had been a popular resort for the leaders of ancient Rome. By the mid seventeenth century a series of villas and gardens had been created there, all of which were positioned on a north-facing slope to look towards Rome. Given the demands of such a site, a pattern emerged whereby the villa would be set on a plateau cut into the hillside, behind which the necessary retaining wall was developed into the major garden feature. At the same time the steeply rising ground could be used to exaggerate perspective in the manner favoured by Baroque designers.

Nowhere was this better achieved than at the Villa Aldobrandini in the creation of the water theatre for Pope Clement VIII (Ippolito Aldobrandini). Among the most munificent of the Frascati patrons, the cost of the aqueduct to supply his garden nearly ruined him. Aldobrandini's architect was Giacomo della Porto, but the most vital contribution to the garden was made by two of the Renaissance's most skilful water engineers, Giovanni Fontana and Orazio Olivieri. The dramatic effect is increased by the positioning of the amphitheatre immediately behind the villa rather than at a distance across a traditional formal garden and the extending of its semicircular wall beyond the limits of the villa. Highly decorated with pilasters and busts set in niches, and surmounted by a balustrade, the theatre wall is dominated by five huge niches, the two on either side containing statues with single jets rising from basins in front. The central figure is a monumental Atlas hidden by a curtain of water pouring down from the base of his globe. Above him on the central axis the balustrade is decorated with the Aldobrandini emblem of a star from which water jets up like a feather to fall on to the figure below. The sweeping extent of the theatre is emphasized by the contrast of the steep water staircase above cut between the thick natural *bosci* of the hillside and rising up to twin spiralling pillars which frame the vista above.

Ironically, perhaps, it was away from the Roman sphere of influence,

The figure of Fame dominates its setting at the top of the main vista at the Villa Garzoni, Collodi.

in the gentler setting of the hills north of Lucca, that the Italian Baroque garden arguably achieved its zenith, at the Villa Garzoni, Collodi. The garden was begun in the mid seventeenth century and represented a radical departure in design by being detached from the villa (built to replace an ancient fortress) to take advantage of the steeply sloping ground to one side. Dense *bosci* separate garden and villa, which looks out over the garden's lowest level. It is the combination of unashamed architectural theatricality and the animation of water which give the Villa Garzoni its individuality. The architectural focal point is the set of three terraces, connected by flights of balustraded stairs and so planned as to give maximum dramatic effect, for above the terraces rises a cascade of roughly hewn stone, hemmed in by hugely tall clipped evergreens and widening as it ascends to give an illusion of even steeper ascent. It reaches the upper pool of the garden between great recumbent female figures representing the cities of Lucca and Florence, with their attendant panther and lion; this pool is enclosed by cypresses and fed by a spout from the trumpet of the figure of Fame, beyond which the garden merges imperceptibly into the hillside woods. Looking down, the dizzy descent of the cascade appears to drop without break over the terraces to the contrasting flat parterre at the lowest level planned around two large circular pools with tall central fountain jets.

The treatment of water in the gardens of the Villa Garzoni has a discernible link with the main features of the Villa d'Este, the Villa Lante and the Villa Aldobrandini. As an expression of the Baroque, the garden of Isola Bella positioned close to two other islands in the Gulf of Borromeo which extends off Lake Maggiore, represents a new stage in the water garden. The dramatic settings of the lakes of northern Italy, the great expanses of water with villages looking up towards the towering distant backcloth of the Alps, inspired a number of superb gardens all benefiting from the wonderful clarity of air and light, combined with the openness and reflective qualities of the lake surfaces. At Isola Bella Count Carlo Borromeo decided to transform the whole island into a floating villa and garden, designed in such a way as to give the impression that the whole was set upon the surface of the water, both when looking out from the island or when viewed from any point on the mainland.

Borromeo began work in 1630 and the gardens were virtually completed by 1670, although work on the rest of the island continued long after. The garden rises in ten terraces from the water level at the western end of the island and continues around both sides. The steep ascent is counterbalanced by the broadness of the upper terraces, which extend back to cover much of the island before merging towards the villa and out-buildings at the western end. The only specific water feature of significance is the fantastic nymphaeum-like water theatre on the second from the top terrace. However, the garden's extraordinary effect derives mainly from the interplay of the broad ascending terraces and the dramatic vertical silhouettes of the enormous array of statues, obelisks and other ornaments, all hugely exaggerated when seen against the surrounding lake. Looking downwards from the upper terraces in any direction there appears to be no break between balustraded retaining walls and the surrounding water. The statues positioned on the very edges and corners of the structure, or even thrust further into the air on pedestals, appear to be effortlessly suspended against the blue background. Here, water is not manipulated by technical brilliance or guided through the garden to enliven architecture; instead, it is the garden's whole canvas, the setting to which every detail relates.

By the early seventeenth century the influence of the Italian gardens was spreading steadily into the rest of Europe and, with it, the emphasis of water features. These were often reproduced faithfully sometimes to the point of dullness – first in neighbouring Austria and France and beyond, in the German principalities, England, and to a lesser extent, the Netherlands, Spain and Portugal. In Austria, where very few gardens were created before the end of the seventeenth century, the only major garden to survive from the early years of the century, Hellbrunn to the south of Salzburg, which survives in its virtual entirety, is faithful to the Italian Renaissance both in overall style and the individual water features.

Created by Markus Sittikus von Hohenems, the cultivated Archbishop of Salzburg who had first hand knowledge of Italian gardens, and designed by an Italian, Santino Solari, the archbishop's castle was joined to the garden by a grotto dedicated to Neptune, alive with water-powered automata, such as singing birds, and *giochi d'acqua*. Other features included a Roman theatre and a large marble table with a central water channel, with the humorous aside of water jets issuing from the table's marble seats. An avenue of water jets led to the Grotto of the Crown or Midas's Grotto, where a crown was lifted into the air on a jet of water.

Where the Italian influence spread to Spanish gardens, it was often merged with a Moorish/Christian style, exemplified in Charles V's

Water jokes, or giochi d'acqua, *were among the most popular features of Italian Renaissance gardens and were imitated in many other countries. At Hellbrunn in Austria seats spouting water around a stone table imitated a similar feature at Pratolino.*

redesign of the Alcazar in Seville. His son Philip II then built the monumental Escorial palace and monastery, where an intriguing combination of styles was effected in the Patio de los Evangelistas, built around an Italian-inspired octagonal temple with four square Moorish-style basins at its corners and statues of the four evangelists set in niches.

The most decisive and direct connection, however, came in the person of Cosimo Lotti, an Italian who had been involved in the creation of the Boboli Gardens in Florence. He came to Spain in 1628 and was commissioned by the cultured Philip IV to transform the gardens of the royal hunting lodge at Aranjuez, which were situated on an island surrounded by the river Tagus. Lotti added a number of elaborate Italianate fountains, in particular the Hercules fountain, modelled on the Isoletto in the Boboli, and the Triton fountain (subsequently moved to the royal palace in Madrid). Although the Aranjuez gardens were subsequently altered, certainly throughout the seventeenth century their fountains were the major attraction for visitors, one remarking that it was impossible to 'cross an avenue, to step into a hut, or walk on a lawn or terrace, without passing five or six basins with statues'. Later, Lotti was to work on the gardens of another royal hunting lodge, El Pardo, where he demonstrated the extent to which he was abreast with developments in Italy by designing the garden's main terrace wall as a theatre wall, with arched niches enlivened with water jets and a spectacular central water staircase.

It was in France, however, that the stylistic influence of the Italian Renaissance was strongest, forged not only by geographical proximity, but also by territorial ambitions and also by the ties of marriage between a number of leading dynasties. Equally significant, she was developing steadily towards becoming the most influential power in Europe, to a position where, by the mid seventeenth century she had assumed the role of major influence in garden style throughout the continent. As we shall see in the subsequent chapter, the influence of Italian gardens was initially considerable, fusing with the indigenous traditions of the medieval moated château to bring about the evolution of French gardens from the medieval to the Renaissance and to assume their own particular identity in the era of the great formal French gardens. Thereafter, the twin influences from Italy and France, with their essentially contrasting but mutually complementary use of water, were to dominate the development of formal water gardens throughout the Continent.

THE FORMAL USE OF WATER *on a grand scale was a major characteristic of the flowering of the French classical garden. Although the designers of the Islamic and Italian gardens had incorporated formal water features into their layouts, it was the great gardens of Versailles, Vaux-le-Vicomte and Chantilly which showed how water, controlled to unite classical architecture and landscape, could become a formidable representation of man's mastery over nature. The energy of the water features in the Italian gardens became in the French classical garden an evocation of power, manifested in formal stretches of water and statuary. While very few later water gardens could rival their French predecessors in scale, the arrangement of such devices as canals and fountains as links between architecture and horticulture came to dominate Western formal garden design.*

The Villa Pisani, Stra, is notable for its formal canal which runs between the house and the elaborate stable block, seen here in the background.

75

Features of the Formal Water Garden

An ornamental bassin *with statuary at Versailles.*

Canal

Historically, the canal was the most important of all large-scale water features, appearing particularly in the gardens of ancient Egypt, Rome, Islam and post-Renaissance Europe, notably in the classical gardens of France, the Netherlands and Germany. No other water feature can impose a comparable sense of large-scale order on a landscape design; when laid out in conjunction with decorative ornamental features or positioned as the centre-piece along a vista through woodland, notably in the French gardens of the seventeenth century, the effect was uniquely impressive. Ideally suited to flat terrain, canals were often built in naturally boggy sites where the necessary depth of water could easily be collected. They have also been built for a variety of practical purposes as well as for their ornamental qualities, forming the boundaries of a garden, as was often the case in the Netherlands, or providing the link between areas of formal garden around a house and the surrounding landscape.

Bassin

The formal ornamental garden pool, usually either square, circular or rectangular, may sometimes be used as a reservoir to supply water for plants or to flow through a garden in channels. In Mughal gardens pools were designed to give a sense of spaciousness and to provide reflections. They were also put to similar use in the great French classical garden.

Buffet d'Eau

The *buffet d'eau* is an interesting small-scale ornamental feature perfected in formal French gardens and designed for niches. Water appears out of a spout to flow over an architectural feature and into a collecting trough or bowl; the surrounding walls are often richly decorated.

A buffet-d'eau *at Chantilly, a much favoured feature of classical gardens.*

The canal at Courances.

Étang

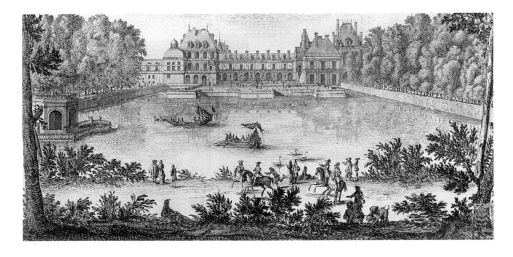

Etang can be defined as a natural pond or lake incorporated into an ornamental garden design, usually with its edges formalized into a regular shape. The most famous example is at Fontainebleau, where a lake was formalized into a trapezium shape to form the central feature of the garden's original layout.

The étang *of Fontainebleau.*

Grille d'Eau

The *grille d'eau* is a series of water jets or fountains aligned to form a screen; this feature was introduced into both Islamic and Western classical gardens and subsequently adapted in later periods. Impressive *grilles d'eau* were made at both Vaux-le-Vicomte, where a series of ascending fountain jets was called the 'Grilles d'Eau', and at Versailles along one side of the large Bassin de Neptune. A large-scale twentieth-century version can be seen at Longwood in the United States. On a smaller scale but equally effective was the screen of water that Geoffrey Jellicoe made during the 1930s at the end of the main parterre at Ditchley Park; the jets of water provided both a vertical feature along the vista and a screen for bathers in the pool immediately beyond.

A section of the moat at Vaux-le-Vicomte.

Moat

The ancient defensive system of water surrounding a building was adapted to use in classical gardens to great effect, nowhere more so than in France. Indeed, the tradition of the moated château was one of the primary sources of inspiration for the French classical garden, and its retention and adaptation is illustrated by a progression from Chantilly to the classical zenith of Vaux-le-Vicomte and later French gardens such as Cany and Courances. The moated castle has influenced the style of gardens in the Netherlands, Germany and northern and eastern Europe.

The grille d'eau of Longwood, Pennsylvania.

Pool

In some instances 'pool' is interchangeable with 'pond', but as a garden feature the pool is generally formalized in shape – circular, oval, or polygonal. As a pond is smaller than a lake, so a pool is smaller than a *bassin* or canal, although the differences between such features is generally as much to do with their surroundings within a garden as their individual scale. A pool may be taken to signify a small- to medium-sized formalized area of water, more often still than disturbed by water from a fountain. It has been one of the most basic and widely used water features throughout gardening history.

A formal pool at Wardington Manor, Oxfordshire.

Swimming Pool

While ablution pools were an important feature of Islamic gardens from their earliest creation in Persia, and lavish public baths were built throughout the Roman Empire, the swimming pool is essentially a twentieth-century addition to the garden. Many early examples built during the first half of the century were in the same style as formal ornamental pools and often highly architectural with sweeping flights of stone or marble steps and ornamental decoration. In recent decades, however, as they have become more widespread, they have often become more functional. Their shape has provided the opportunity for adventurous design, as in the work of Thomas Church in California, and in many instances they provide the centre-piece for a plan combining water, architecture in the form of a changing-house, and planting.

The swimming pool at Antony House, Cornwall, has been made into a formal water feature within the total garden design.

Water Parterre

A water parterre is a feature in which water in basins and pools replaces or is integrated with the intricate pattern of flowerbeds, low hedges, paths and lawns of conventional parterres. In Italian Renaissance gardens, where there was often a strong downward progression of water from an upper point, they often formed the lowest level of the garden, contrasting with the terraced treatment above, as in the gardens of the Villa Lante and the Villa Garzoni. They were equally well suited to the flat sites of classical gardens in France, the Netherlands and Germany. One of the most impressive of all examples is the Grand Parterre laid out by Le Nôtre at Chantilly.

A contemporary engraving of the water parterre of Chantilly, 1671–72.

Water Wheel

Probably the largest example of this supremely important engineering device ever built was the Machine de Marly, incorporating fourteen huge water wheels which raised water from the Seine to supply Versailles.

The Machine de Marly.

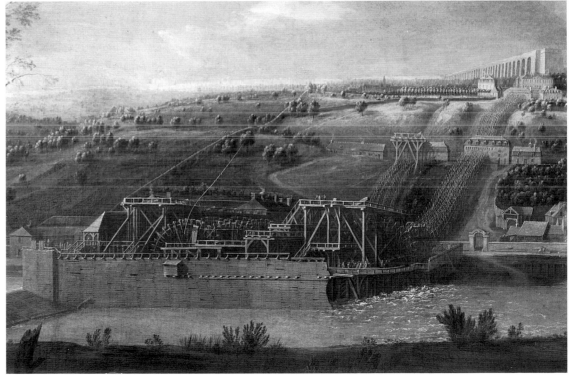

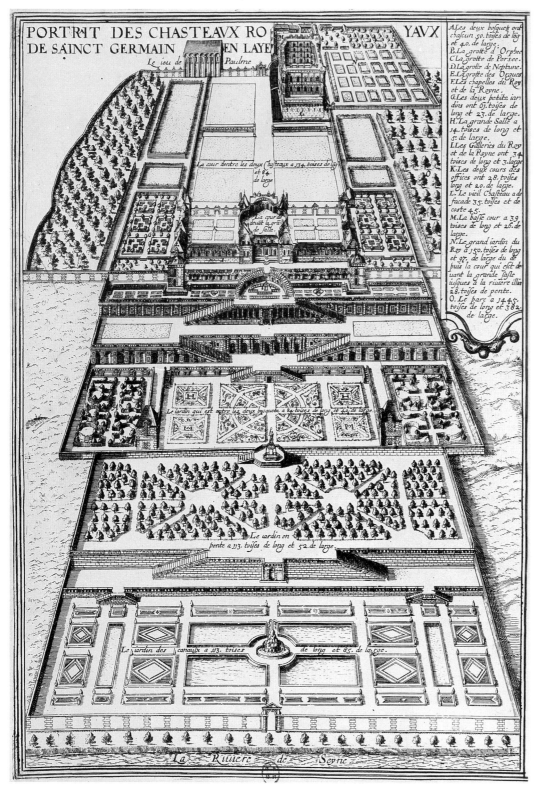

PORTRAIT DES CHASTEAVX RO   YAVX
DE SAINCT GERMAIN   EN LAYE

Le ieu de   *Paulme*

A.Les deux bosquets ont
chascun 50.toises de log
et 40. de large.
B.La grotte d'Orphe.
C.La grotte de Persee.
D.La grotte de Neptune.
E.La grotte des Orgues
F.Les chapelles du Roy
et de la Royne.
G.Les deux petitz iar-
dins ont 63.toises de
long et 23.de large.
H.La grande Salle a
14.toises de long et
5. de large.
L.Les Galleries du Roy
et de la Royne ont 34.
toises de long et 3.large
K.Les deux cours des
offices ont 28.toises
long et 20. de large.
L. Le vieil Chasteau a de
façade 35.toises et de
coste 45.
M.La basse cour a 39.
toises de long et 26.de
lagge.
N.Le grand iardin du
Roy a 150. toises de long
et 97. de large du de-
puis la cour qui est ie-
uant la grande Salle
iusques a la riuiere illa
28.toises de pente.
O. Le parc a 1445.
toises de long et 382.
de large

La cour dentre les deux Chasteaux a 114.toises de log
et 84.
de large

La cour
deuất la grũ
de Salle

Le iardin qui est entre les deux bosquets a 84.toises de long et 40.de large

Le iardin en
pente a 113.toises de long et 52.de large.

Le iardin des canaulx a 113. toises   *de long et 85. de large.*

La   Riuiere   de   Seyne.

An engraving of 1614 by Alexandre Francini, showing the garden of Saint-Germain-en-Laye, where he and his brothers designed the waterworks.

The Formal Water Garden

5

NOTHING illustrated better the centrality of water in the evolution of gardens and its infinite adaptability than the progression from Renaissance to Neoclassical and the influence of Italian craftsmen on garden design in France. Just as the two styles were represented by differing interpretations of ornament, architecture and horticulture, so their moods were encapsulated in their use of water. In the former, the sheer variety of water features seems to express the vibrant confidence and sense of discovery of the Renaissance and man's ability to enjoy a central but harmonious position in nature; in the latter a sense of power, the power of absolute monarchy, and man's ability to subjugate nature is suggested by large, formal expanses of water, creating seemingly unconfined reflections and vistas. The move towards this style of expression was at first tentative and related to the development of the relationship of the French château and its garden. Its ultimate success was demonstrated by the progression from the angular, seemingly unconnected canals of the early Fontainebleau gardens to the awe-inspiring symmetry of André Le Nôtre's Vaux-le-Vicomte.

The Italian influence on French garden design can be traced very precisely through the story of the Francinis, a family of craftsmen who specialized in water features. Within one generation of moving from Italy to France they had adopted the name of de Francine and had progressed from being leading figures among the hydraulic engineers of the Italian Renaissance to being responsible for the waterworks in the royal classical gardens of seventeenth-century France. Thomas Francini, after some involvement in the creation of the waterworks of Pratolino, left Italy in the late 1590s with his brothers Alexandre and Camille to work for French king Henri IV. Their first major project for the king and Marie de Medici, his wife, was the royal garden at Saint-Germain-en-Laye, which became the supreme French Renaissance garden. Thomas devised the system of fountains, the ornate grottoes in the garden and the water-powered automata, including a woman playing the organ in one grotto, Mercury blowing into a shell and a dragon beating its wings. He also built the aqueduct to bring water from outside the city of Paris to the

The French Classical Garden

Le Nôtre's majestic creation at Vaux-le-Vicomte; an important aspect of the formal design is the reflection of the house in the pool behind.

An engraving of 1661 by Israel Silvestre of the great cascade in Cardinal Richelieu's garden at Rueil, on which were modelled the later cascades in the royal gardens of Saint-Cloud and Chantilly.

Luxembourg gardens where Marie de Medici aspired to emulate the Boboli Gardens of her native Florence. Alexandre Francini's major work was at Fontainebleau, where perhaps his most famous addition was the monumental Tiber fountain built for Henri IV and positioned at the centre of the garden's main parterre; he remained at Fontainebleau to organize the waterworks and fountains.

By the time of Louis XIII, whom Thomas had amused as a child by building models of the fountains at Saint-Germain-en-Laye, he had been elevated to the official rank of 'Superintendent of the Waters and Fountains of France'; after the death of Henri IV in 1610, he was also able to work outside the royal patronage, for the minister and enemy of Marie de Medici, Cardinal Richelieu. The cardinal's garden at Rueil was specifically designed to rival the royal gardens and became one of the most admired of the period; Louis XIV is reputed to have sent Le Nôtre there before he began work at Versailles. Francini's major contribution was to bring in water by aqueduct over a distance of two kilometres, and to plan the great cascade which inspired later ones such as that at Saint-Cloud, the garden's canals, fountains and two enormous grottoes.

While the major axis of the garden, the Grande Allée, with the cascade pouring down at one end and incorporating a canal and the two grottoes, looked forward in design to the sweeping vistas of Le Nôtre, the ingenuity of Francini's water features clearly show their Italian, Mannerist inspiration. The interior of one grotto was described by Elie Brackenhoffer after a visit in the mid seventeenth century, 'In four of the angles there are satyrs, in the other four nymphs, all life-size, prettily formed of sea shells and snails; each character makes a strange gesture with the hand, sometimes putting a finger on the thigh, sometimes on the mouth, while the other hand directs the *membrum virile* in the air and water spouts from it; on four sides there are fountains with fine oval basins; near each stand three marble figures also discharging water from their genitals. In the middle stands an octagonal marble table on which one could do all kinds of amusing things, in that by pressing the instrument or tube coming from the centre, one made all kinds of figures with the water, for example lilies, cups, flowers, glasses, moons, stars, parasols.'

Thomas's son, François, who changed the family name to de Francine, succeeded to his father's official position and worked with his brother Pierre as his deputy, organizing the efficient operation of the bewildering quantity of waterworks which filled the royal gardens during the reign of Louis XIV. Without doubt the major task – probably the greatest engineering challenge to face any garden designer – was to maintain the supply of water at Versailles from the famous Machine de Marly.

The French architect Philibert de l'Orme is usually credited with first stressing the importance of both modifying the original defensive role of moats into a decorative one and of the necessity of draining the marshy ground surrounding many châteaux by the creation of ornamental canals. He did this at Anet, created between 1546 and 1552 for Diane de Poitiers, the mistress of Henri II and rival of his wife Catherine de Medici. After much extension, the gardens of Anet were finally altered beyond all recognition in the early nineteenth century, but de l'Orme's design was of immense influence in the manner it drained a previously useless site into canals that provided ornamental surrounds to the ambitiously symmetrical arrangement of the château and its axial, rectangular gardens.

A more famous surviving legacy of Diane de Poitiers, in conjunction with the later work of Catherine de Medici, is the château of Chenonceaux which remains the most vividly romantic French example of harmony between architecture and water, without the later sophistication evident in classical gardens.

The château was built in 1515 on the site of an ancient mill standing in

A contemporary engraving of Henri IV's Diana fountain at Anet by Jacques Androuet du Cerceau.

Chenonceaux, where the river Cher was harnessed to provide the dramatic setting for the château, is completely surrounded by water and has gardens on either bank of the river.

the river Cher. François I gave the château to Diane de Poitiers (whom he had chosen as his son's mistress) and she commissioned the five-arched bridge linking the château with the river's far bank and a new garden (no longer in existence) which she made there. After the death of Henri II, however, Diane de Poitiers was summarily ousted from Chenonceaux by the now all-powerful Catherine de Medici, determined to exact her revenge. She commissioned the completion of the château's design by building the gallery wing across the existing bridge, thereby extending the château across the full extent of the river. In the final picture the water was used to best advantage as a setting for the château itself and provided the link with the elaborate gardens on both banks of the river – which survive on one bank with their dividing and surrounding canals on either side of the approach forecourt. The basic structure of the arrangement has remained unaltered, thereby retaining its strongly Renaissance character, blending the medieval and romantic in architecture and setting.

Elsewhere, notably at Fontainebleau and Chantilly, there is a clear progression in the work of successive hands from the Renaissance to the classical which was largely effected by the varying use of water. Fontainebleau, whose name derives from 'fontaine bel eau', after the natural spring in the huge forest where the royal seat and town were sited, was a favourite place of François I and it was he who began the development of the garden around the château which he altered and extended. A triangular lake was made out of a marsh to one side of the raised causeway which approached the château from the forest, forming the central area of the gardens and accounting for their originally angular layout. Moats were built along many of the château's main façades, enclosing much of the building. But in much of their detail François' gardens were distinctly Italianate. Classical statues cast by Vignola were positioned in the main courts of the château, while another Italian, Primaticcio, designed the Grotte des Pins, the first architectural grotto in a French garden, in one corner of the Jardin des Pins planted by François.

The style of the first Fontainebleau gardens was kept by Catherine de Medici, though she made changes to the ornamental features, and it was not until the time of Henri IV that a clear shift in the garden's whole style and emphasis appeared. Decorative features continued to be added, notably the Diana fountain in the small enclosed courtyard garden on the north side of the château, but the major area of change was on the opposite side of the causeway from the triangular lake, where François' Grand Jardin was made into the Parterre du Tibre, named after the

fountain by Alexandre Francini positioned in the centre. On either side of the fountain a canal divided the parterre and formed the line that was subsequently developed into the Grand Canal; this was begun in 1609 and extended along a majestic axis from the garden out into the forest.

Henri's work was finally brought to its conclusion by Le Nôtre, with the assistance of the younger de Francines; the Grand Canal was enlarged to its present size of 1145 metres long by 39 metres wide and in the retaining wall of the parterre at one end an elaborate cascade was built. The canal transformed the whole scale of the gardens and linked them convincingly to the surrounding forest. Le Nôtre further emphasized this effect with an axis at right-angles across the Grand Jardin, greatly simplified into four squares around a large square central basin and leading to an even larger circular basin jutting out into the forest but divided from it by a moat. The development of the garden from a series of essentially Renaissance enclosures and closed vistas to a classical, outward-looking landscape was thus completed.

By the standards of seventeenth-century France, Chantilly was not an enormous château and this fact, combined with the relatively large size of the moats, has always accentuated the importance of the water features. When Le Nôtre was commissioned by the Prince de Condé (whose family acquired Chantilly in 1643) to replan the gardens, he could not

The Tiber fountain (above) by Alexandre Francini at Fontainebleau and a plan of the château and gardens in an engraving by Jacques Androuet du Cerceau.

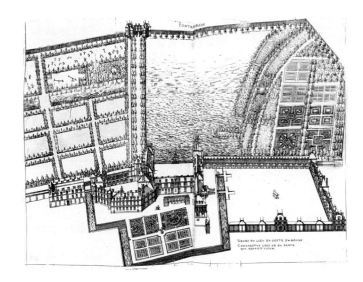

Water features, including a canal, were an integral part of Le Nôtre's design at Vaux-le-Vicomte (above); the extraordinary unity of the whole scene is revealed when viewed from the château, where formal planting and bassins *make up a wholly satisfactory design (opposite).*

satisfactorily produce a design of axes in which the château itself would not be the central point. Using Montmorency's terrace as the link between château and garden, Le Nôtre opened up a vast north-south vista extending in one direction from the terrace across the old moat and on along an avenue cut through the forest, and in the other across a new parterre garden to where the new Grand Canal crossed at right-angles and extended away in both directions.

Le Nôtre took full advantage of the abundant natural water of the site. From the monumental flight of steps descending from the terrace the parterre is completely dominated by water: beyond a first central circular *bassin* the main wide canal fills the central area of the garden and ends in a semi-circle. On either side rectangular compartments are virtually taken up with symmetrically arranged circular and oval *bassins* around larger central rectangular ones. The Grand Canal was produced by formalizing an existing small river and greatly increasing its potential volume of water by a circular collecting pool at one end falling into a second, hexagonal pool. From here the canal – nearly a hundred metres wide – stretched for over a mile, crossing the parterre canal near its centre, before turning an angle and extending for a further distance of some half-a-mile.

The château was rebuilt on the original site during the nineteenth century, having been destroyed during the Revolution, and all the main features of Le Nôtre's garden survive. Exactly as Le Nôtre – who himself considered Chantilly possibly his best work, given the limitations of the existing site – intended, the overriding impression is that the château is completely enveloped by water, both immediately and within its far larger-scale surroundings, from which canals also lead into the countryside beyond.

Le Nôtre may have considered Chantilly his greatest work, but arguably his finest achievement, made even more remarkable by the fact that it was his first, was Vaux-le-Vicomte. Here, between 1556 and 1661, in the creation of the surroundings for a new château built by Louis Le Vau for Louis XIV's finance minister, Nicholas Fouquet, Le Nôtre adapted the long-established French ideal of a moated château to the new demands of classical landscape.

The garden descends almost imperceptibly in a broad sweep through terraces, before rising away at the far end to a statue of Hercules silhouetted on a distant hill. Woods on either side provide the framework for this scene of harmony and order, in which the essential components joining château and landscape in one design are sculpted ornaments in

LES III.FONTAINES.

At Versailles innumerable fountains and groups decorated the bosquets *flanking the main central vista and both sides of the palace (*above, opposite above *and* below*).*

logical, symmetrical sequence, the patterned detail of *parterres de broderie,* and water. In the great flat expanses of the parterres the various *bassins* were positioned so that reflections brought the vital element of verticality to the scene and at the same time emphasized the overall scale and proportion; for instance, the rectangular *miroir d'eau* on the central axis reflects the full façade of the château. In comparison to what was to come at Versailles, fountains were used sparingly at Vaux-le-Vicomte, for the major aspiration of the garden was the balance of its whole rather than the individuality of its parts.

In addition to the *bassins* in the parterres, then, the most important water features were the canals along the garden's cross-axes which represented the subtlest part of Le Nôtre's scheme and were to be the completing factor in the major classical landscapes. In the progression away from the château, the initial cross-axes where the level changes from one parterre to another are of secondary size compared with the *tour de force.* This lies ahead, concealed by a more pronounced drop, while the main canal stretches across the garden for nearly 1000 metres, its length and size acting as a perfect foil to the garden's primary axis. Centrally positioned on the far side is the grotto of seven huge arched niches, surmounted by a balustraded terrace beyond which the ground rises to the Hercules. The surprise of the canal's appearance, the effect of the grotto and the sound of the great buttressed cascade on the château side seemingly lessens the status of the château itself as the focal point of the garden. Yet, if one looks back from the terrace above the grotto to the view of the château raised on its water-enclosed platform, it is immediately clear that the whole effect is so proportioned as to enhance the position of the house.

The scale of Le Nôtre's vision as a landscape designer is best demonstrated at Versailles. The major plan of the gardens was completed between 1662 and 1668, before Louis XIII's modest château had been transformed into the vast palace by Le Vau and Jules Hardouin-Mansart. The final design, after decades of additions, saw the basic layout of cruciform axes aligned on the points of the compass hugely embellished but fundamentally unaltered. The whole scheme, in which Le Nôtre collaborated constantly with architects, sculptors and hydraulic engineers, was a symbolic representation of power imposed on the landscape and expressed through classical allegory. The water features were crucial to the success of the whole scheme.

The Versailles landscape was unique not so much because of its great area, but because of its combination of scale, exemplified by the vast cruciform canal, and richness of detail, achieved in the series of fountain *bassins* and their sculptural groups. Without water, such a vast landscape would have lacked life; water was the agent that not only brought the sculpture groups in the fountains to life, but also brought together the palace and gardens through the reflections thrown back by the expanses of the various *pièces d'eau*.

Looking from the Parterre d'Eau across the front of the palace, the gardens' central allegory on Apollo the Sun God is revealed in the main series of fountain *bassins*, from the Bassin de Latone, Apollo's mother, in the upper part of the gardens, to the Bassin d'Apollon, where the Sun God's chariot rises from the water in a scene of consummate drama. Beyond, on the main axis, lies the great canal; on either side of it, terminating the cross-axes and enlivening the wooded *bosquets* which frame the central vista, the fountain *bassins* continued the garden's iconography. These include the Bains d'Apollon, representing sunset, the Bassin du Dragon and beyond, on the same axis, the enormous Bassin de Neptune, together forming two of the most spectacular groups. Each enclosed *bosquet* had its own water feature, such as the water theatre, the water colonnade and the children's fountain.

The surroundings of Versailles, however, were not endowed with limitless water supplies and over the years a series of hugely ambitious schemes were devised to satisfy the demands of the 1400 fountain jets and the additional volume required for the larger displays, such as the Bassin d'Apollon, to be effective. The construction of the Machine de Marly – which eventually was transferred to feed the cascade in Louis's newer garden at Marly – has been described, but earlier there had been an extensive system of pumps followed by an attempt to drain the water-table to a series of collection points. Most ambitious, but eventually abandoned, was the plan to construct an enormous canal of over 100 kilometres from the river Eure; this required a high aqueduct at Maintenon which was the only part of the project carried out, the ruined arches surviving today.

*The Bassin de Latone at Versailles
(left) stands between the Parterre d'Eau
in front of the palace and the Tapis Vert.
Beyond is the garden's most powerful
fountain group of Apollo in his horse-
drawn chariot, rising from the water
(right), while yet another water feature
combined with elaborate statuary forms
the foreground of this view towards the
Orangerie (above).*

French Influence

Following the example of Le Nôtre at Versailles, Philip V of Spain used water features to provide grandeur and spectacle in the garden of his palace at La Granja, Segovia (above, opposite left *and* opposite right*).*

LOUIS XIV'S VERSAILLES was the model which garden makers all over Europe aspired to throughout the rest of the seventeenth century and most of the eighteenth. Classical formality was dominant and virtually without exception the desired effect was achieved by the use of water in partnership with sculpture and architecture, and in many cases in the setting of broad elaborate parterres. In each country the French influence was grafted on to national traditions and adapted to varying terrain.

Frederick the Great once remarked that 'a young man passed for an imbecile if he had not stayed for some time at Versailles'. Louis XIV's grandson, Philip V, was brought up in France as the Duke of Anjou and later became King of Spain, determined to emulate his grandfather's garden in his new country, at La Granja near Segovia. The mountainous setting north of Madrid could hardly have been more different to that of Versailles and in the end the garden's character derived from both the grand French style that Philip aspired to and the Italian influence of his wife, Elizabeth Farnese. The site determined that the predominant feature would be a vigorous display of water rather than grandiose serenity. Certainly Philip was determined that nothing would thwart his ambitions; over the years some 5,000 men were employed creating his gardens, many of them hacking out terraces with picks and aided with gunpowder. The best of the team of sculptors were all pupils of Le Brun and had worked in the royal gardens of France. Their skills were reflected in the superb quality of the lead figures of the fountains and the white marble free-standing figures. Water was collected from the surrounding mountains into two enormous reservoirs, the Mar and the Estanque Cuadrado.

At the top of the cascade, originally aligned with Philip's private apartments, stands a pavilion built, like the palace, of distinctive pink Segovia granite and white marble. In front, the Fountain of the Three Graces feeds the cascade descending in ten broad steps of white marble and jasper to the Fountain of Amphitrite. Like the *tapis vert* at Versailles, the cascade is flanked by alternating statues and urns set back on either side. Parallel to the cascade, the Carrera de Caballos is a series of five descending circular pools with a total of 114 jets. The highest jets spring from sculpture groups in the centre of each pool: at the top, Andromeda and Perseus and, at the foot, Neptune surrounded by sea-horses. The highest jet in the garden and at one time the highest in the world, rises to a height of 50 metres from the Fountain of Fame and demonstrates the water pressure achieved in the direct gravity feed to the fountain from the Mar reservoir. In the final analysis, one wonders how much Philip, renowned for his melancholy disposition, appreciated the splendours of his garden, for when the cascade was completed he is supposed to have remarked, 'It has cost me three millions and amused me three minutes.'

In turn, La Granja inspired the most monumental cascade made anywhere in the world, at the Palazzo Reale, Caserta, near Naples, the work of Philip and Elizabeth's son, Charles III, after he had acquired the throne of Naples. The design of the gardens around his new palace was the work of a Neopolitan architect, Luigi Vanvitelli and, after his death in 1773, the work was continued to his design by his son Carlo. On one side the palace faced on to a piazza surrounded by formal parkland. On the other side an axis was created between avenues stretching for a distance of some three kilometres upward to a steep hillside. The cascade and water staircase were laid out between the hill and the palace, descending in stages to basins decorated with sculpture groups. The vast conception was made possible by an aqueduct that brought water from a mountain source 40 kilometres away. In the end, though, the sheer scale proved too ambitious and some of the detail, notably the sculpture groups of the basins, remained uncompleted. The gruesome nature of the work involving slaves was immortalized in a carved relief of them shackled together on the balustrade above one of the main fountain basins: garden ornament can have a serious message.

*The taste for formal features of enormous scale in garden design reached a peak in
the Grand Cascade at the Palazzo Reale, Caserta (above and opposite).
The group of figures at the foot of the cascade enacts the
story of Diana and Actaeon.*

This eighteenth-century engraving shows the French-style cascades and fountains at Peterhof.

The cascade emerges from the hillside and drops over rough boulders through natural wood to the first basin where the twin sculpture groups of Diana and Actaeon are positioned on either side of the central flow. From here the progress of the water is formalized into a more gentle descent in stages; first disappearing underground to re-emerge into a basin with a fountain surmounted by Venus at the head of the first water staircase. At the foot of this the water again flows underground to reappear in a second similar basin with a sculpted fountain and then flows on down a second stairway, the descent of which is in broader, gentler stages, before feeding into a long canal and thence into the largest of the basins, which celebrates Juno and has a high retaining wall with niches and sculpture at the foot of the canal. The final result is perhaps the most extreme example of formalized water being used to make a single dramatic statement in landscape.

Elsewhere in Italy the French influence produced a limited number of large classical gardens, all dominated by water features, of which perhaps the most impressive to survive is the Villa Pisani, created for the Doge of Venice, Alvise Pisani, between 1735 and 1756. The villa is positioned on the edge of Stra, immediately inland from Venice. Through the centre of a broad vista cut between woodland a canal stretches right to the far end where its water reflects the central portico of the magnificent stable block's Palladian facade, stretching between the trees on either side. The only decoration along the length of the canal are pairs of classical statues positioned on the water's low retaining walls.

Such restraint was not always evident in the attempts to emulate Versailles and nowhere did engineering skill and ingenuity combine with lavish decoration more forcefully than at Peter the Great's Peterhof. Here again the connection with France was directly personal, for the guiding hand behind the creation of the garden was Jean-Baptiste Alexandre Le Blond, a pupil of Le Nôtre and already a distinguished garden designer in France before he left in 1716 to work for the Russian emperor.

As in all similarly ambitious gardens the key to success was sufficient water supply, which came via a specially built aqueduct from a source in hills over 20 kilometres away. The whole system and the distribution of water through the gardens was devised by the hydraulic engineer, Vasily Tuvolkov. Basins in the upper park, on the landward side of the palace beyond the main forecourt, collected the water which was then piped beneath the palace to emerge at the head of Le Blond's double cascade. This is built of white marble steps and falls along the central axis from the palace's balustraded terrace, the water flowing into a semi-circular basin followed by a straight canal cut through a tree-lined vista to the sea. Set on pedestals at the descending levels of the cascade are gilded statues of classical gods and heroes alternating with urns; in the centre of the basin set on a rocky island is the gilded figure of Samson forcing open a lion's mouth from which issues an enormous jet of water. The canal is lined with single-jet fountains in small circular basins; set in the *bosquets* on either side are more hidden fountains and smaller cascades.

One of the earliest German gardens was that at Herrenhausen, begun in 1680 and extended a decade later, for Sophie the wife of Ernst, Elector of Hanover. She had been brought up in the Netherlands, while Martin Charbonnier who designed the gardens, was French; the Grosser Garten undoubtedly reflects these twin influences upon the orderly Germanic plan. Because of the absence of canals within the main garden, water does not immediately dominate the layout, but is used rather to hold together the complex symmetrical pattern.

The central canal at Peterhof stretches from the foot of the cascade in front of the palace to the sea.

*At Herrenhausen, Hanover, water falls in ordered steps down the balustraded
retaining wall of the garden's main terrace (*opposite*). The tall jet of a fountain
enlivens one of the long formal vistas (*above*).*

Fountain basins are a major feature in the main parterre in front of the palace at Herrenhausen.

The Dutch influence is immediately evident in the canals lined with trees which completely enclose the stiffly rectangular garden. The development of the site, which covers fifty hectares, was in two halves; the first an intricate parterre which centres on a single round basin. In the second half of the garden, a star-shaped *bosquet*, the treatment is different but equally geometrical, formal fountain basins hold together the pattern of vistas in a far more prominent manner. In the centre is the main fountain basin with one enormous jet; around it are four smaller basins with single-jet fountains forming an exact square with interlinking vistas at all angles.

At Herrenhausen the use of water in the garden was restricted to tying together the axes of the garden's regimented pattern, but in the two gardens of Max Emanuel, Elector of Bavaria, Schleissheim and Nymphenburg, its role was far more prominent. Again, the gardens reflect the twin Dutch and French influences. Max Emanuel had served as Governor of the Spanish Netherlands, while the designer of the Schleissheim garden, Dominique Girard, came from Versailles. Here the garden was laid out between the existing *Schloss* and a new building, the Lustheim. The central axis of the garden was formed by a wide canal and subsidiary canals enclosed the perimeter of the whole garden. The most unusual feature of the garden was the semicircular canal which enclosed the Lustheim and its parterre.

Girard was also involved in the larger garden of the elector's summer residence, the Nymphenburg, begun in earnest after Max Emanuel returned from exile in 1715. As at Schleissheim the source of water was the river Würm and the garden focused upon a long central canal, on one side of the palace extending away towards the town, on the other beginning in a large basin on the edge of the parterre in front of the palace and continuing away between formal *bosquets* to a basin into which fell a large cascade. The parterre itself was planned around a series of nineteen ornate fountains. The largest and most decorative of these was the central octagonal fountain of Flora made of white marble. The garden's most intriguing feature was the manner in which a series of perimeter canals linked up to give the impression that the palace and parterre were detached on an island.

These gardens were all laid out on flat sites, ideally suited to an elaborate combination of parterres, fountains and canals. Dramatically different was the hillside site of Wilhelmshöhe, where the Landgrave of Hesse-Kassel was inspired by a visit to Italy in 1700 to build perhaps the most extraordinary cascade in existence. With his Italian architect,

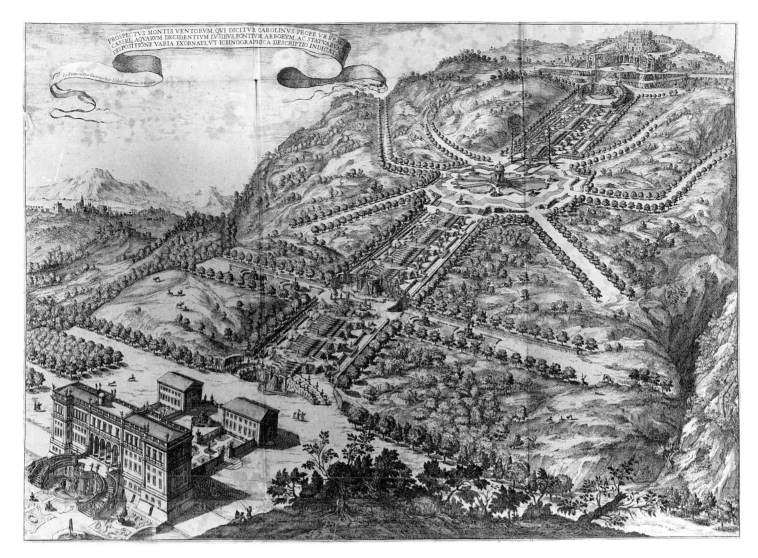

PROSPECTVS MONTIS VENTORVM, QVI DICITVR CAROLINVS PROPE VRBEM
CASSEL. AQVARVM DECIDENTIVM LVSIBVS, FONTIVM, ARBORVM, AC STATVARVM
DISPOSITIONE VARIA EXORNATI, VT ICHNOGRAPHICA DESCRIPTIO INDICAT.

Io. Franciscus Guernerius Nihil Romanus Delineavit.

Giovanni Guerniero, the Landgrave planned to transform the steep hillside of the Karlsberg rising behind his newly-built palace with a vast series of cascades and grottoes, the extent of which can be gauged by the fact that only the upper section, covering less than a quarter of the total distance, was ever completed. On top of the hill Guerniero built a monumental octagon containing a reservoir, rising into a pyramid nearly a hundred feet (30 metres) high and surmounted by a thirty-foot (9-metre) bronze copy of the Farnese Hercules. The giant's club was so large that it could contain eight men. From the octagon, the water tumbles down the initial cascade built of rough boulders for over a hundred feet (30 metres) before feeding into the formalized stairway of the main cascade which descends to a large basin which was as far as the grandiose design was ever extended.

This 1706 engraving by Alessandro Specchi of Wilhelmshöhe, Hesse-Kassel, shows the huge array of intended cascades, of which only the upper third was completed.

Nymphenburg, Bavaria; the garden was planned in the early eighteenth century according to the French taste, although some Dutch influence can be discerned in the use of canals (below).

The foot of the dramatic cascade at Wilhelmshöhe; the garden was begun according to a formal design in the early part of the eighteenth century, but Picturesque elements were added later.

The Dutch Formal Garden

Canals, fountain basins and cascades all went to make Het Loo the most decorative of Dutch gardens (above and opposite).

THE DUTCH AS A NATION – and as gardeners – came into their own in the early seventeenth century with the retreat and eventual disappearance of Spanish control of the Low Countries and the growth of wealth and power built upon the trading empire of their East and West Indies companies. The evolution of the Dutch garden during this period is uniquely interesting because in the essentially bourgeois republic the development and design of gardens was not, for the first time since the Roman empire, solely the prerogative of the ruling and aristocratic classes.

The high point of the Dutch classical garden was achieved by Prince Frederick Hendrik when he began laying out a new garden around Honselaarsdijk in 1621, sadly completely destroyed at the end of the Napoleonic Wars in 1815. The rebuilt castle and its forecourt formed a rectangle enclosed by a moat; extending away on three sides in strict proportion were the gardens, also enclosed on all sides by canals. The proportions of both moated castle and gardens were the classical 3:4, and the repetition of the water enclosed castle and garden marked one of the purest applications of classical theory to garden design. The garden was arranged in regular compartments along a strong open central axis and continued on the far side of the castle to form the approach lined by avenues and canals. This was to be a hallmark of Dutch garden design and one which was unquestionably influenced by developments in France.

The garden at Honselaarsdijk was modified by Prince William of Orange, later King William III of England, and his English wife Mary; indeed, their reign witnessed the height of French influence in Dutch gardens, characterized by clearly Baroque features. The style was most impressively displayed at Het Loo, whose garden was laid out in the late 1680s and the 1690s. It survives today in an immaculately restored state. The gardener there, Daniel Marot, was a Huguenot who left France in 1685 and was largely responsible for the development of the Franco-Dutch style so appreciated by his royal patrons.

At Het Loo the pure classicism and water-enclosed design of Honselaarsdijk has been replaced by something equally geometric in plan, but with an altogether more ebullient spirit expressed mainly in its fountains and cascades. On either side of the palace, below the respective royal apartments, were the King's and Queen's Gardens, while the main garden was laid out in two areas stretching away to the north. The first, a large rectangle called the Lower Garden, was a novelty in Dutch gardens in that it was sunk below raised terrace walks on three sides. Its eight beds were filled with *parterres de broderie* arranged on either side of a strong central cross-axis dominated by water features. In the centre was the Venus fountain containing an eponymous white marble figure set in an octagonal white marble basin with gilded tritons and sea-dragons all spouting water. On either side the pairs of square beds were centred upon fountains of the terrestrial and celestial globes, while at either end the cross-axis terminated against the terrace walls in cascades named after Narcissus and Galatea.

Immediately beyond a further cross-axis, marked by avenues originally planted with oaks and flanked by narrow canals, lay the Upper Garden whose symmetrically curving boundaries terminated in semi-circular colonnades. The centre-piece of the Upper Garden was the most spectacular of all the water features, the King's Fountain, where water spouted 13 metres high from the centre of an octagonal basin. It says much for Dutch engineering skill that the water for such a powerful jet was drawn from a natural spring.

By the end of the seventeenth century the gardens of Het Loo were among the most famous in Europe and, with the accession of William III to the English throne in 1688, the Dutch style inevitably spread to England where the amount of earlier Italian and French influence had to some extent been limited by the Civil War and Protectorate. Nonetheless, it was these continental influences which effected the transition from the Tudor garden to the Renaissance garden during the early decades of the seventeenth century. Of prime importance was the work of Salomon de Caus, a French Huguenot who had travelled in Italy and gained detailed knowledge of gardens there before moving to England in 1610 to work for Queen Henrietta Maria and her son Henry, Prince of Wales. Much of de Caus's work was preoccupied with water features, in particular grottoes, automata and decorative fountains. In 1615, two years after leaving England to work for James I's daughter, Elizabeth, on the creation of the garden at Heidelberg in Germany for her and her husband, the Elector Palatine, he published *Les raisons des forces mouvantes*, which discussed the theory and practice of hydraulics for water systems in gardens.

The sculptural fountains of Het Loo are among the garden's finest water features (above). The Cascade of Galatea at Het Loo, with the corresponding one of Narcissus, forms the end of the main cross vista of Het Loo's Lower Garden (opposite).

The English Formal Garden

BY THE TIME of the restoration of Charles II in 1660, he and a great number of English aristocrats had spent years in France in exile. Almost inevitably, the royal gardens at Hampton Court, St James's and Greenwich were soon redesigned around long formal canals. That at Hampton Court was the most impressive, stretching away between double lime avenues, but it was the subsequent addition by William III of the Great Fountain Garden in the semicircle immediately in front of Wren's new part of the palace which really completed the garden. The thirteen fountains in Marot's *parterre de broderie*, the whole semicircle enclosed by a narrow canal, provide a point of contrast with the main canal which stretches away through the park.

No English garden ever boasted water features on quite the scale of those of the French gardens; lavish ornamental classical fountains seemed not to be fully to the national taste. One surviving exception to such reticence, however, is the cascade at Chatsworth where gardening innovations were to occur again in the future. The cascade was created for the first Duke of Devonshire who rebuilt the house and surrounded it with extensive formal gardens. The parterres were laid out by George London and Henry Wise and animated by fountains designed by a Frenchman, Grillet, who had been a pupil of Le Nôtre.

The house's Baroque character was perfectly complemented by Grillet's cascade, laid out at right angles down the steep hill to the east and aligned with the south façade. The downward stream of water emerged from a cascade house built by England's most individual Baroque architect, Thomas Archer; the combined effect continues to make the cascade the most vibrant water feature in any English garden.

The comparatively reserved formality of the Dutch garden seemed very much in tune with English taste and a number of gardens were laid out around canals in the 1690s and during the first decade of the eighteenth century. Only a few, however, have survived the sweeping changes of the Landscape Movement. At Hall Barn in Buckinghamshire the poet Edmund Waller used a wide canal as the link between his house and the formal woodland garden of *allées* that he created at the far end of the water. At Bramham Park in Yorkshire a T-shaped canal was designed as an integral part of a French-inspired woodland garden.

Perhaps the most interesting Dutch-style water garden to survive is Westbury Court in Gloucestershire, which was completely restored by

This view of Chatsworth (opposite) shows the fountains which adorned London and Wise's formal garden; Archer's domed cascade house is visible in the foreground; it has survived with its cascade and remains as strong a feature as when it was originally built.

the National Trust after 1967. The garden was first laid out by Maynard Colchester between 1694 and 1705 and subsequently added to by his son. The water of a small stream, the Westbury Brook, was diverted to feed a canal, at one end of which was built an unusually tall gazebo and at the other a wrought-iron *clairvoyée* was let into the garden's brick boundary wall in a style common in Dutch gardens. The combination of the formal water, the flat site and the contrastingly vertical gazebo gave the garden a strong Dutch character which was retained by Colchester's son when he added a second canal parallel to the first and extending at one end into a T-shape.

The Westbury garden almost certainly influenced that at Frampton Court which stands just across the Severn estuary from Westbury, where a similar canal was laid out in the early eighteenth century and later given the distinguished terminus of a castellated Gothic summer-house built in 1760, reputedly by Horace Walpole. In neither garden, however, were

Dutch influence was strongly in evidence at both Hampton Court (above) and Westbury Court, Gloucestershire (right).

The evolution of Chatsworth's garden has seen the steady addition of new water features alongside the old (left above, centre and below). Paxton's Emperor fountain (above), however, remains one of the most impressive.

the canals arranged axially within the main façades of the houses, as would have been the case in most Dutch gardens and certainly in the French gardens which influenced the architect John James in the design of his home Warbrook House in Hampshire. James filled a position of considerable influence in eighteenth-century English gardens after his publication in 1712 of the English translation of *La théorie et la pratique du jardinage* by A.-J. Dezallier d'Argenville, which advocated the formal principles of Le Nôtre. At Warbrook the French influence can be clearly seen in the canal which James cut through woodland on an axial line with his new house's central pediment. James's publication demonstrated that formal gardening, with its attendant water features, continued to be popular in England during the early decades of the eighteenth century. At the same time, however, developments were gathering pace that would produce a very different style derived from the fusion of garden and natural landscape.

Nineteenth-century Formal Gardens

THERE WAS MUCH of private gardening in the nineteenth century, notably in Victorian England, which combined the formal classicism of Italy and France with obvious characteristics of the period, notably lavish and grandiose display. This was most forcefully demonstrated in vast and intricately decorated parterres and in fountain basins where the primary concern seemed to be monumental size. In some cases, Witley Court for instance, Victorian industrial ingenuity was harnessed to garden planning in the form of the steam pump, though at Chatsworth the long-established method of a gravity-powered water supply was used.

Many of the great Victorian parterre gardens, with flower-beds surrounding fountain pools and the whole decorated with balustrading, urns and statuary, were laid out as foregrounds to an existing landscape park. In these cases, of which Trentham and Harewood House are two of the outstanding examples, the result was an effective juxtaposition of formal water features in the foreground with the distant view of a 'Capability' Brown lake.

Chatsworth was in the vanguard of Victorian gardening developments, thanks to the partnership of the sixth Duke of Devonshire and his head gardener Joseph Paxton. Paxton became head gardener in 1826 and devised and supervised spectacular additions over the next two decades. One of his major achievements was to preserve continuity so that his nineteenth-century additions could be enjoyed alongside the seventeenth-century cascade and 'Capability' Brown's eighteenth-century landscape in which the judiciously enlarged river Derwent was given increased prominence by the new approach to the house which crossed the river via a three-arched bridge. Among Paxton's earliest additions were water features in the wooded hillside above the house and in main gardens. He constructed enormous naturalistic rockworks over some of which water fell in the cascade of the Wellington Rock and most impressively from the great height of a broken aqueduct.

These were all complete by 1843 when, with the prospect of a visit to Chatsworth by Tsar Nicholas I of Russia, Paxton constructed the Emperor fountain in the long canal pool to the south of the house. The single fountain jet was fed by water from a specially built reservoir covering eight acres and situated high up in the woods to the east; the pressure threw the water 88 metres (290 feet) into the air. At the time it was the highest fountain jet in the world and although, in the event, the Tsar's visit did not take place, the fountain completed a memorable view that takes in the towering jet and the Sea Horse fountain, both aligned with the south front of the house.

The great Victorian parterres were often planned either with a series of fountains, as at Trentham Park, Staffordshire (left), or with one monumental group, as at Holkham Hall, Norfolk (above).

Paxton's fountain at Chatsworth was unadorned by sculpture and impressed purely by its colossal height, but elsewhere the prospects of similarly grand country houses were enriched by far more lavish, Italian-inspired groups, notably those at Holkham Hall and Castle Howard. Both houses were given new parterres during the 1850s, laid out by William Nesfield in front of their main façades. At Holkham the parterre extends into a central balustraded semicircle containing a fountain basin with St. George and the Dragon carved in stone by Charles Smith. At Castle Howard, Nesfield laid out the formal garden to the south of the house and was influential in the design of the enormous central fountain group of the kneeling Atlas supporting the globe, surrounded by four Tritons. All the figures are over life-size and carved in stone; the water, which sprays from the top of the metal globe, from the Triton's conches and from the rich shellwork and other decorations of the basin, was driven by a steam engine.

Fountains provided a marvellous outlet in garden design for the Victorians' industrial and engineering entrepreneurship, their admiration for Italian and French classicism and their enjoyment of enormous size. Spectacular while it lasted, the combination was relatively short-lived in British garden design. In the United States similar conditions

Italian and French gardens, and their abundant use of water in particular, provided the inspiration for a series of grandiose gardens created in the United States around the turn of the twentieth century. Three of the most lavish were Longwood in Pennsylvania (left above), Biltmore House in North Carolina (left) and Vizcaya in Florida (opposite).

Vizcaya reproduces an Italian Renaissance palace and garden to remarkable effect.

were making themselves felt by the end of the nineteenth century, resulting in the creation of even more lavish water gardens.

In 1906 the industrialist Pierre S. du Pont bought the Longwood estate in Pennsylvania where a series of formal gardens were laid out in the setting of extensive surrounding woodland. Most impressive of all was the fountain garden, with its series of jets giving an impression of perpetual motion and mirrored by the glass of the great conservatory to one side. The Longwood waterworks emulated both the Italian style and the splendours of Versailles. A few years later at Vizcaya in Florida, another industrial magnate, James Deering, consciously recreated an Italian Renaissance villa and garden on the edge of Biscayne Bay. The harmony of water and architecture that was the cornerstone of the Italian originals is faithfully reproduced, whether in the fountains of the oval entrance courtyard or the main sweep of terraced gardens to the south which incorporate a water staircase and a succession of pools. The overall effect is heightened by the water of the bay sweeping around the garden and forming part of the vistas in various directions.

During the last quarter of the nineteenth century French gardens witnessed a strong revival in acclaim for André Le Nôtre, led by a father and son partnership, Henri and Achille Duchêne. One of their first major commissions was the restoration of the parterres at Vaux-le-Vicomte for Alfred Sommier, who had purchased the château in 1875. During the years before the First World War Achille Duchêne restored the gardens of Courances for the de Ganay family to produce a formal water garden that has been widely admired ever since.

The château of Courances and the original garden dated from the seventeenth century; it was the spirit of that period which Duchêne recaptured with his designs, using the plentiful supply of water from natural springs and from the river Ecole. A long canal between avenues of plane trees approaches from the north, leading to the château raised up above the moat which surrounds it. Beyond the château the central axis continues from a formal parterre to a perfectly positioned rectangular *miroir d'eau*, terminating in the figure of Hercules reflected in a circular *bassin*. To one side a series of gentle cascades leads to the river, canalized to flow in suitable formality through its woodland setting. In addition to the restored features, Duchêne added a number of new ones, including a horseshoe-shaped canal and a circular basin to one side of the château. Throughout the garden there is exceptional harmony in scale between the architecture of the château, the formalized woodland setting and the omnipresent water.

The success of Courances and other French gardens led to commissions overseas for the Duchênes; one of the most ambitious of these was the creation during the 1920s of the water parterre at Blenheim Palace for the Duke of Marlborough. Before the First World War Duchêne had already laid out the parterre on the west side of the palace, but this second commission was far more demanding, since it had to provide the link between the west side of the palace and the great expanse of 'Capability' Brown's lake. Duchêne's design suited both the situation and the Duke's desire for grand formality in the palace's immediate surroundings. Two terraces were linked in a manner reminiscent of Vaux-le-Vicomte by twin flights of steps in a retaining wall with five central arches. The upper terrace was the larger one, square with a pattern of basins and low scrollwork hedges, while the lower one was rectangular with twin rectangular pools. In one of these he placed a fountain modelled on Bernini's River Gods fountain in Rome, which had previously been in the cascade in the park; in the other the centre-piece was an obelisk. As for the Duke, the end result pleased him sufficiently for him to declare to Duchêne that 'the ensemble of terraces is magnificent and in my judgement far superior to the work done by Le Nôtre at Versailles'. Whether Duchêne agreed or not, it was the highest praise possible from his patron.

A plentiful supply of natural water prompted Achille Duchêne's masterly recreation of a seventeenth-century formal garden at Courances (above and left).

*Among Duchêne's most ambitious designs was the water parterre at Blenheim Palace, Oxfordshire, filling the foreground between the palace and 'Capability' Brown's lake and the park beyond (*opposite *and* above*).*

Twentieth-century Formal Gardens

BEFORE THE FIRST WORLD WAR formality was the predominant characteristic of a majority of gardens and a number of outstanding water gardens were created in England, including Buscot Park in Oxfordshire and Athelhampton Manor in Dorset. Buscot was designed between 1904 and 1911 by Harold Peto and while the garden clearly illustrates his admiration for Italian classicism, it is also a highly original and ingenious response to the specific requirements of the site, enhancing the relationship between existing house and landscape. The requirement at Buscot was to provide a link through woodland between the house and its large lake some 250 yards away to the east. Peto's response was a narrow vista cut through the mature trees through which water flows in a gentle, often imperceptible descent towards the lake. The varying shapes of successive pools linked by canals contrast with the narrowness of the vista.

The garden at Athelhampton Manor was laid out earlier than Buscot by Francis Inigo Thomas and is an important example of the recreation of a period atmosphere in sympathy with the architecture of the sixteenth century house. Water had always been a feature of Athelhampton, for the river Piddle encloses two sides of the garden; it provided the source for Thomas to plan his series of intimate formal enclosures linked by the view from one fountain to another. The main vista descends from the large Great Court to the small circular Corona and beyond to the Private Garden. The varying scale of each is complemented by their three different pools, while the vista between the fountains provides a strong sense of unity. From this main axis are others at right-angles and the variations from one to another are emphasized by the contrasting treatment of water, from the spouting lion mask in a small area beside the Corona to the long canal which extends along the same axis as the rectangular pool of the Private Garden and the garden front of the house.

At Athelhampton and Buscot, Thomas and Peto were creating new gardens in established settings, a common enough combination in twentieth-century garden design. In contrast, Edwin Lutyens was often given the opportunity to design new houses and their gardens simultaneously. In his garden work – and, indeed, in his early approach to architecture in general – he was greatly helped by his partnership with Gertrude Jekyll. The water features in the gardens laid out during the years of their most active collaboration up to the First World War were designed with her approval if not active involvement. In a number of

*P*ools and fountains make up the centre-pieces of each enclosed area in the Edwardian garden of Athelhampton Manor, Dorset.

*H*arold Peto's fervent admiration for the formal garden tradition found its most satisfying outlet at Buscot Park, Oxfordshire (opposite) which was laid out during the first decade of this century.

The tank pool (above right) which Sir Edwin Lutyens designed to fill the right-angle between the existing house and his new addition at Folly Farm, Berkshire, has a distinctly Islamic aspect. The formal canal (above) along the axis to the house's main façade was one of his favourite devices and one that he repeated at Abbotswood, Gloucestershire, where the dipping-well (opposite) is typical of his enjoyment of vernacular detail.

their most successful gardens, for instance Folly Farm in Berkshire, the complex arrangement of component areas is emphasized by the varying formal treatment of water.

Folly Farm is at its most impressive on the side of the house where the canal garden extends away from one façade, complementing the Dutch style of Lutyens' architecture. Immediately against the house, where the steeply pitched roof descends to curving buttresses which line a two-sided loggia, the position of a square water tank immediately against the loggia appears almost Islamic in its fusion of architecture and water in an enclosed area. Quite different is the octagonal pool and its central brick and stone island with alternate curving and straight sides in the centre of the rose garden, the focus of the detailed geometric design. A further contrast is presented along one side of the rose garden where a simple walk between yew hedges leads away from the house to a circular fountain basin decorated with stone shells.

Lutyens demonstrated great skill in the integration of rectangular canals and square water tanks into his designs, realizing at the same time the capacity of such water features to provide a restful contrast to often intense architectural and planting detail. Almost invariably, they were decorated with an architectural feature that gave them immediate originality: the curving retaining wall out of which water flowed through a series of square recesses, with flanking flights of right-angled square

steps, at one end of the Folly Farm canal; or a vaulted semi-circular wall-spout, a device which he used on many occasions, notably in the gardens of Abbotswood, Gloucestershire, and the Deanery Garden, Berkshire. Later in his career, after the watershed work on New Delhi and no longer in partnership with Jekyll, the monumental classical designs of Gledstone Hall, Yorkshire, and Tyringham, Buckinghamshire, were dominated by enormous formal canals. Tyringham is one of the most striking twentieth-century Neoclassical garden designs, its canal sweeping away from the house built by Sir John Soane for 300 yards to the garden's edge. At one point the canal is broken by a circular pool on whose axis Lutyens built matching domed pavilions to echo the dome of Soane's house.

Tyringham was a 'pure' water garden in the long established sense that water and architecture came together so successfully that horticultural embellishment was superfluous. However, most of Lutyens' earlier commissions had confirmed the far more prevalent twentieth-century tendency of water features being part of a varied pattern. This is well illustrated at Dumbarton Oaks, Washington, the masterwork of the American Beatrix Farrand, where over a period of twenty five years from 1920 she designed the gardens for her friend and patron Mildred Barnes Bliss.

Mildred Barnes Bliss was inspired by her knowledge of the great classical gardens of France, and twentieth-century gardens have constantly recalled the past water glories of France and Italy, if only rarely matching their scale. In those instances where features have been created on a magnificent scale, such as the sweeping loggia and man-made lake created by W.W. Astor at Hever Castle during the first decade of the century, or the equally impressive temple and Neptune pool of the Hearst garden made by William Randolph Hearst at San Simeon in California during the 1920s, the revivalist element predominates. In less grandiose schemes such influences from the past have often been more subtle and effective. In some instances, revivalism has also been combined with highly original modern design; a good example of this is Blue Steps at Naumkeag, Massachusetts, designed by Fletcher Steele and part of a diverse garden created before and after the Second World War, the sweeping lines of the double flights of steps and slender handrails over small arched cascades clearly indicate the influence of the Renaissance, while their construction in concrete, bright blue colour and setting with white-stemmed birch trees flanking both sides are all distinctly of this century.

This fountain group (opposite) *forms a focal point at one end of the Pebble Garden at Dumbarton Oaks, Washington, created by Beatrix Farrand. The smaller fountain* (above) *in the same garden reinforces the impression of a garden shaped by water features.*

The garden of Compton Acres, Dorset, was created between the First and Second World Wars; its coastal position encouraged the maximum use of water to evoke the theatrical feeling in each of the different areas, which range from the Italian style to the Japanese (left, above and opposite).

The Mughal inspiration for the unique garden of Sezincote, Gloucestershire, is continued throughout the garden. In the main area a descending stream which widens into a series of large ponds is the central feature of the design, which combines lush planting with Indian-inspired ornament and architecture.

At Heale House, Wiltshire (above) abundant water from the river Avon fills the little streams of the Japanese garden; the arched bridge and thatched tea-house were built by Japanese craftsmen at the beginning of this century.

Geoffrey Jellicoe's water garden at Shute House, Dorset (opposite) descends from rich planting in its upper reaches to a series of Mughal-inspired pools with bubble fountains surrounded by grass below; a statue acts as a focal point.

Italy and France may have been the most widely favoured places of inspiration, but the formal water garden has also proved the ideal medium for introducing to the West the particular flavour of gardens from different parts of the world – be it Japan, China, or the Islamic countries. The early part of this century, for instance, witnessed a considerable fashion for Japanese gardens. At Heale House, Wiltshire, where the river Avon forms the boundary on two sides and provides abundant water, the flow was channelled into one of the most ingenious Japanese gardens of the period. The garden's quality no doubt resulted from the years that Heale's owner, Louis Greville, had spent in Japan; its *tour de force* is the thatched tea-house beneath a Japanese wooden bridge.

At Compton Acres, Dorset, created after the First World War, the geographical variety of the gardens is more varied, with the inclusion of Italian and Japanese water gardens. Strikingly different is the canal garden laid out to one side of Sezincote, Gloucestershire, the unique early nineteenth-century house in which the architecture of Mughal India is fused with the English classical tradition. During the late 1960s Sezincote's owner, Lady Kleinwort, commissioned Graham Stuart Thomas to design the formal Mughal garden. This has a canal extending from the house and a path at right-angles which centre upon a raised, octagonal fountain basin in a style wonderfully suited to the architecture of the house; a curving orangery extends along one side to an octagonal pavilion.

The Mughal garden also inspired some of the formal water features in the garden of Shute House, Wiltshire, designed from 1970 by Geoffrey Jellicoe in partnership with Shute's owners Michael and Lady Anne Tree. The garden at Shute is dominated by water in the form of the series of natural springs and pools which mark the source of the river Nadder. In one place Jellicoe designed a narrow rill, descending first via small cascades and then in a contrastingly quiet manner from a series of formal pools, each with a central gravity-fed bubble fountain. Perhaps most important, however, is the element of variety in the garden at Shute, displaying the distinctive tendency in twentieth-century garden design to combine water features in both formal and natural styles. From its source, the water flows in one direction to be canalized into formality, emphasized by the Palladian arched grottoes at the far end, beyond which it then flows underground and turns to feed the top of the cascade. In another direction from the source, the atmosphere is quite different, as paths wind around dark natural pools overhung with trees, a transformation described by Jellicoe as being from the classical to the romantic.

*PepsiCo Park, New York, provides a number of examples of how formal water features are effective in a Modernist style (*above *and* opposite*): the Dolphin fountain by David Wynne is a uniquely exciting feature in its combination of a dynamic sculpture and vigorously activated water.*

THE PRIORITIES *of 'natural' garden design, most famously expressed in the English Landscape Movement of the eighteenth century, were the achievement of harmony with the surrounding natural landscape and the representation of an idealized natural setting. The English park, perfected in the designs of 'Capability' Brown, was a deliberate composition in complete keeping with its context, shaped by the presence of water features on a major scale. Although often contrived, the whole effect was designed to recreate nature as faithfully as possible and so the sinuous, unpredictable line of lake and stream replaced the geometry of canals and water parterres as the ideal form of water in the garden.*

William Kent's Venus Vale in the garden of Rousham House, Oxfordshire.

Features of the Natural Water Garden

Bath House

Originally built during the Roman Empire as essential architectural features of the public baths present in most towns, bath houses were incorporated into Roman villa gardens. In many ways they were the ancient equivalent of the modern swimming-pool pavilion which, when transported to the seventeenth-century Villa Garzoni, had an even closer resemblance, with divided areas for men and women. The classical origins made bath houses fashionable architectural features for English eighteenth-century landscape gardens. William Kent added one at Rousham which, together with the octagonal pool it overlooked, was known as the Cold Bath; at Painshill the connection was even more direct in Charles Hamilton's Roman Bath. Perhaps most interestingly, 'Capability' Brown broke with the classical tradition when building two of the most attractive of all bath houses, one in Jacobean style overlooking the lake at Burghley, and a second, Gothic building at Corsham Court.

Boat House

The lakes of landscape gardens throughout Europe were often embellished with boat houses, which combined practical use with pleasing architectural appearance. The strong tradition of boating on the lakes of water gardens in both China and Japan ensured their popularity in the garden design of those countries. In public parks, where recreation has always been a prime consideration, they have often been the only – or at least the most prominent – architectural features, following Paxton in Birkenhead Park.

The boat house at Wardington Manor, Oxfordshire.

Bridge

The bridge was undoubtedly the most important architectural feature to have been developed in conjunction with water, its utilitarian purpose often overshadowed by its symbolic importance and surface decoration. National styles have been quite distinctive, such as the Chinese moon bridge with a central arch, whose reflection completes a circle, and the arched wooden bridges of Japan.

Bridges were not a prominent feature in Islamic gardens, the gardens of the Italian Renaissance or classical France. They were, however, a mainstay of the English Landscape style, often the only architectural feature adorning a landscape of water, trees and parkland and usually built to the highest standards. Most prevalent were simple stone three- or five-arched bridges, often of impressive size and occasionally decorated with balustraded rails or with statues or urns. The Palladian bridge, with colonnades and pediments, represented a peak of decorative architecture for the garden; three examples survive in England at Stowe, Wilton and Prior Park.

In landscape parks throughout Europe false bridges were sometimes used at the end of a stretch of water to give the impression that it continued further. During the twentieth century painted wooden bridges in a variety of styles, ranging from Gothic to 'Chinese Chippendale', have become widely popular and have proved adaptable to gardens of all sizes. Throughout history bridges have most often been built of wood or stone, although wrought and cast iron has been used for decorative railings.

A variety of bridges: Palladian at Stowe (above), and wooden at Spring House (below left) and Heale House (below right).

Lake

Whether natural or man-made, lakes were especially important to gardens in the Landscape style and the gardens of China and Japan. In both these latter countries water has been celebrated in its natural state and lakes have often been focal points or a major feature in large-scale gardens. In Japan the traditional stroll gardens usually progress around the irregular edges of a lake, the path unveiling a series of different views and features along the way. In China lakes covering many hundreds of acres were created by building dams; in imperial gardens, for instance, the extent of lakes was seen to represent the ruler's power, while at the same time they were often seen to be symbolic of the sea, especially when dotted with small islands which were the destination of boating expeditions.

In English landscape gardens the lake often presented an image of serenity which, by virtue of its size, also represented the status of its owner. Since the nineteenth century lakes have been used as centre-pieces of extensive waterside planting, especially in the United States.

The lake at West Wycombe, Buckinghamshire.

An informal pond at Upton House, Oxfordshire.

Pond

Together with lakes and streams, ponds are one of the three naturally occurring water features most commonly incorporated into gardens. In the contemporary garden they are rarely left unadorned and their banks are usually enlivened with waterside planting. The digging of a pond is often a satisfactory way of converting a small area of boggy ground to make a far more desirable garden feature.

Rill

The rill, a narrow channel of water, is often used in garden design to give an impression of naturalness by following a winding course. Something of a curiosity and only really given prominence by the famous example made by William Kent at Rousham, which has been taken to express Hogarth's sinuous line of beauty in a form acceptable within the classical context of early eighteenth-century landscape gardens. From the main Octagon pond of the Venus Vale, Kent's rill – originally wider than as it survives today – winds through woodland to the Cold Bath, another feature with classical overtones.

A stream amid informal planting at Wilhelmshöhe.

William Kent's curving rill at Rousham.

Stream

Streams are an important feature of Oriental gardens; water in the natural state is treated with great reverence in both China and Japan. Where space does not allow a real stream in the Oriental garden, this may be expressed by a far smaller arrangement of stones and flowing water or by rocks and sand. In Chinese gardens a stream would enter from a set point and only ever flow through the garden in one direction. Where the water entered a garden, it was often dramatized into a waterfall and the points of entry and exit were both traditionally disguised to give an impression that the stream continued in both directions. For many centuries streams were frequently formalized in European gardens into flowing canals, but their natural attractions returned with the advent of the landscape movement in the eighteenth century. During the twentieth century they have provided the settings for some of the most attractive contemporary water gardens, the harmony between flowing water and plants being especially effective.

The Natural Water Garden

As a development of what has come to be called the Landscape Movement gathered pace in England during the first half of the eighteenth century, gardens were increasingly merged with their surrounding landscape, as they came to be seen less as formally enclosed areas adjacent to a house and more as compositions on a larger scale. Flower gardening did not disappear, but it did not play a significant role in these landscapes. The revolutionary transition from limited symmetrical formality was effected partly by a changed use of architecture – although in the work of Lancelot 'Capability' Brown this virtually disappeared – but most importantly and immediately in the changed treatment of water. Some superlative landscape gardens were created without any water, but these were extremely rare. At the height of the movement, virgin natural landscape at its most rugged and visually stimulating was taken as the ideal model for garden design. Such scenes most often included a ravine and rushing torrent or a mountainous waterfall, providing an extreme contrast to the artificial water features of earlier gardens.

Although the Landscape Movement is often looked at as a whole school, the leading individual designers had widely varying aspirations which were often best exemplified in their differing uses of water. For William Kent at Stowe the stream named the Styx was an immediate and living reference to classical mythology; Robert Aislabie's choice and subsequent treatment of the valley of the river Skell is a most striking demonstration of a transition from formality to informality which could never have been achieved without the use of water; for 'Capability' Brown the creation of the lake at Blenheim at one stroke created a feeling of harmony between the architecture of the palace, the bridge and the surrounding landscape.

At the Earl of Burlington's Chiswick House the Palladian order of the garden's original layout by Charles Bridgeman and subsequent early embellishment by Kent was more or less preserved. The one substantial alteration was Kent's naturalization of the lines of the formal L-shaped canal and his building of a rustic three-arched cascade at one end of the

The English Landscape Garden

An idealized natural scene: the Gothic temple across the lake at Charles Hamilton's eighteenth-century garden of Painshill, Surrey (opposite); like all the garden's other features, this has been restored. A stone arch makes a dramatic frame for the vista of water at Stowe, Buckinghamshire (above).

serpentine stretch of water in 1738. At Claremont, where he also followed Bridgeman, the latter's large circular pool, overlooked by a grass amphitheatre, was naturalized into a lake and at the same time extended in size to accommodate an island and become the focal point of the garden's winding paths. It was the same story – on a larger scale – at Stowe, where Bridgeman's large octagonal basin, positioned at the end of the central southward axis from the house just before his bastioned ha-ha, was transformed into the Octagon lake, extended eastwards in two arms, one up to the source of water from the Elysian Fields, the other to

The classical ideal in landscapes was beautifully realized both at Stowe (below) and the later garden of West Wycombe, Buckinghamshire, where the Music Temple stands on an island overlooking the lake (opposite).

where the Palladian bridge would later be built. Westwards the water was made to fall over a cascade into the larger eleven-acre lake which Kent made out of a trapezium-shaped pool.

In Kent's most celebrated garden at Rousham the choice of site and design of the water features clearly denote the architect's wish to create a classical landscape in the English countryside. Here again, he followed in the footsteps of Bridgeman who must be credited with the choice of site which took full advantage of two sweeping bends in the river Cherwell and the spur and valley to one side. It was Kent, however, who emphasized the river's integral role in the garden's design by opening up sight-lines from key points: to the distant Heyford Bridge over the river, along the stretch of water between the bends to the Gothicized mill and, in another direction, to an 'eye-catcher'. Within the garden the classical landscape focused upon the Venus Vale, where water descended through a series of four pools linked by cascades and decorated with lead statuary. From the octagon pond at the lower level the garden's most self-consciously natural introduction was the serpentine rill (originally a wider stream) which winds through woodland to the Cold Bath and on to a clearing containing a classical temple.

Henry Hoare had comparable aspirations to create a classical landscape, as Kent had done at Rousham, and at Stourhead he created the eighteenth century's most sublime classically-inspired scene which unfolds around the large lake. Indeed, it is the water features which make the garden a coherent entity. As at Studley Royal, the garden is detached

William Kent's drawing for the Venus Vale at Rousham.

from the house; initially the site was a series of small valleys containing ponds fed by springs that formed the source of the Stour. The building of a large dam brought the water level up to join the ponds into a twenty-acre lake with winding edges which tapers along the valleys into three fingers. Around there Hoare planned his classical landscape to be enjoyed via a set itinerary around the lakeside.

With the exception of the Temple of Apollo, which is set up on a small hill, the other buildings, notably the Pantheon at the far end of the lake and the Temple of Flora whose façade is revealed from the Pantheon, were positioned on the water's edge; a five-arched bridge was built where the lake extends to the dam and the village of Stourhead beyond. The overall effect is one of remarkable unity between the water, classical architecture and the wooded hills on all sides. Perhaps the most ingenious feature is the grotto, lit from above by a light-well in its domed, encrusted ceiling. There is a recess into which a series of springs are channelled to pour out in a cascade beneath the recumbent figure of the nymph of the grot and out of the urn held by the river god.

An eighteenth century engraving of Stourhead, Wiltshire, showing the Temple of Flora and the medieval cross in the distance; the garden was designed around its central lake and is perhaps the most arcadian of all English landscape designs.

Alexander Pope's grotto (above) in his garden at Twickenham initiated a fashion which was followed in many eighteenth-century landscape designs, including Painshill (opposite).

At West Wycombe another gentleman garden designer, Sir Francis Dashwood, created a similarly idyllic classical landscape around the centre-piece of a large lake formed by damming a small stream running through a valley overlooked by the house. The transformation of the house, with its varied Palladian façades, and the steady embellishment with temples of the park on the hillsides around the lake were carried out in progressive stages from the 1730s to the 1780s. Probably the two most significant stages in the landscape's development were the building of the cascade, damming the stream to form the lake, during the late 1730s, and the addition in 1778 of the Music Temple, designed by Nicholas Revett, on the island in the lake. By this time, the initially elaborate cascade had been simplified to flow between stone nymphs and the Music Temple was positioned so that, viewed from below the cascade, it appears to float on the water.

The grotto at Stourhead was among the finest examples of many which were built in English gardens in the first half of the eighteenth century. Their popular classical connotations and suggestions of the fantastic ensure that the revaluation of nature did not preclude them from fashionable taste. One of their most important enthusiasts was the poet Alexander Pope, whose taste in gardening matters was possibly more influential than that of any other man at the time. The entrance into his garden at Twickenham was a tunnel transformed into a grotto from whose watery darkness the visitor emerged. More lavish examples were created by Charles Hamilton at Painshill and Thomas Goldney at Goldney House in Bristol. Hamilton's ingenuity was first shown by the manner in which he raised water from the river Mile via a water-wheel into the small valley where an elongated lake became the central feature of his garden. His grotto, concealed beneath a bridge, was unusually large, its walls and ceiling covered in exaggerated style with crystal stalactites and pieces of mineral off which the water was reflected in agitated fashion. No doubt this created Hamilton's desired effect to 'fill the mind with that sort of delightful horror which is the best genuine effect and truest test of the sublime.' Goldney's grotto was made later than Hamilton's and was especially notable for the small steam-powered pump that forced the water out of an urn held by Neptune, spotlit at the back of the arched cavern by a shaft of light from the ceiling, and into giant shells on the edge of a pool.

Grottoes, temples and, in some gardens, classical statuary were all important and acceptable features in the early landscape designs, where an affinity with the painting of artists such as Claude and Poussin was as

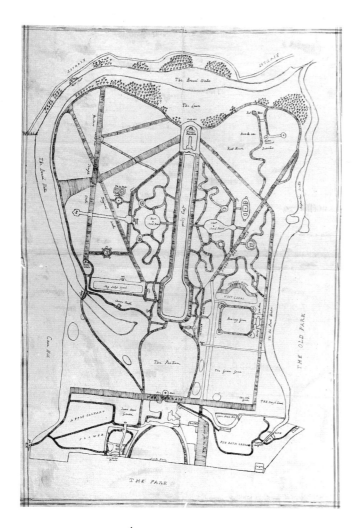

At Wrest Park, seen here in a sketch plan of 1829, the formal central canal of the early eighteenth-century garden, which terminates in Thomas Archer's Banqueting House, was retained when the canals of the surrounding areas were 'naturalized' into streams.

important as the appearance of naturalness. In the work of 'Capability' Brown, however, the creation of landscape was virtually devoid of any such allusions and aimed at the creation of a far simpler aesthetic effect by a synthesis of contoured grassland, trees and water, often on an immense scale; Brown's lakes were designed to give an illusion of endlessness which suited the ambitions of his clients. In many cases, though, the endlessness was hardly illusory; the lake at Blenheim, covering over a hundred acres, was the largest, but many others were of similar proportions such as the one at Coombe Abbey covering nearly ninety acres, made in flat countryside from a tiny brook by excavation and the building of a dam thirty feet high.

The parks designed by Brown used land in a way which was both visually pleasing and made economic sense for his clients. Therefore, where the ground had to be excavated for the creation of a lake, digging was kept to the minimum that would serve to give an impression of depth from any angle; in many cases, especially where the lakes tapered away at their ends, the water was shallow enough for wading. Often a key consideration was the need to combine the draining of poor, marshy ground, thereby enabling it to be used for grazing, with realizing its potential as a natural site for a lake. In 1750, in the first major commission of his career at Croome Court, where he also designed a new Palladian house, he demonstrated the kind of technical ability that would make him lastingly popular with ambitious landowners.

Considering that 'Capability' Brown is usually condemned for the wholesale destruction of the existing gardens on any site that he was commissioned to redesign it is interesting to note here that the limited work he carried out at Wrest Park resulted in the best possible juxtaposition of a retained formal water garden and the naturalization of the peripheral features. The garden was originally laid out after 1706 for the Duke of Kent to a grandiose, French-inspired, formal design of avenues and canals cutting through woodland *bosquets* around a central axis containing the most splendid formal water statement made in any English garden, the long canal which terminates at the domed hexagonal Banqueting House built in 1711 by Thomas Archer, architect of the Cascade House at Chatsworth. Brown was employed by the duke's granddaughter and her husband between 1758 and 1760 with orders that the central canal vista and the formal woodlands were to be retained. Around the perimeters, however, the existing canals were linked up to form a stream curving gently around the garden; beyond the pavilion a large formal pool was naturalized to fit into this gentle, watery plan.

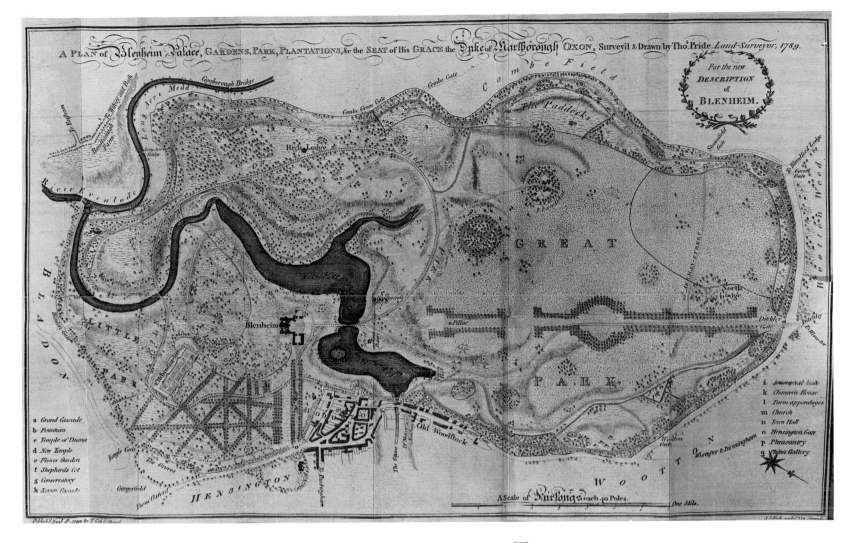

A PLAN of Blenheim Palace, GARDENS, PARK, PLANTATIONS, &c the SEAT of His GRACE the Duke of Marlborough, OXON, Survey'd & Drawn by Tho. Pride, Land-Surveyor, 1789.

For the new
DESCRIPTION
of
BLENHEIM.

a   Grand Cascade
b   Fountain
c   Temple of Diana
d   New Temple
e   Flower Garden
f   Shepherds Cot
g   Conservatory
h   Lower Cascade

i   Newnington Bank
k   Chaucer's House
l   Farm appendages
m   Church
n   Town Hall
o   Hensington Gate
p   Pheasantry
q   China Gallery

A Scale of Furlongs each 40 Poles.   One Mile.

The importance of water in Brown's landscapes is well demonstrated by the situation that confronted him at another early commission, Petworth. The site had no obvious supply of water, such as a stream, and yet the somewhat bland combination of the Sussex countryside and the house's long elegant façade demanded the element of water. Brown employed a technique, which he often repeated, of seeking out small underground springs and diverting their water through underground pipes to feed the lake. Elsewhere, where a lake's creation required the damming of a stream, the desired level of water could be achieved to a very high degree of exactitude, allowing Brown to contour the surrounding land with similar precision.

Once he had achieved the desired water level, Brown also took care to ensure that as far as possible its fluctuations were minimized.

This plan of 'Capability' Brown's park at Blenheim Palace shows the dramatic effect of his damming of the small river Glynde to form the great sinuous lake which is crossed by Vanbrugh's bridge.

Overflow channels were built in stone or brick; in some cases a plug-like device was incorporated so that the lake could be emptied. Other lakes have weirs or even a sort of waste outflow. Puddled clay was used to line the lake beds if the subsoil was not sufficiently waterproof; this was time-consuming and expensive but usually effective. At Harewood House, however, where Brown created one of his most famous landscapes in the 1770s, with the house looking across sloping parkland to the lake, it appears that the lake sprang a leak through a hole 'large enough to bury a horse in' and eventually cost £1,000 to repair.

Much of the visual success of Brown's lakes derived from their irregular shape and the sense of illusion that this gave was often emphasized by his treatment of a lake's furthest extent. The water could be tucked round a corner, so that it appeared to continue, or trees could be planted closely on the bank so that the water was in virtually permanent shadow and therefore its extent difficult to gauge. Equally, a well-positioned island planted with trees, as in the case of Trentham, Staffordshire, would have the same effect of disguising a lake's limit. Occasionally one of the few architectural features Brown incorporated into his designs, a false bridge, was positioned as an eye-catching feature

This engraving by Paul Sandby of Brocket Hall, Herefordshire, shows the lawn gently sloping to the water's edge and Paine's bridge in the background – a quintessential eighteenth-century scene.

at the end of a lake, perhaps the most unusual being the wooden bridge with Ionic columns that he built at Scampston Hall in Yorkshire.

Indeed bridges were the most frequent architectural additions to Brown's parks and at Chillington they are used to particularly masterful effect. The lake – covering seventy-five acres and one of Brown's largest – lies on one side of the park and is approached along a narrow winding stream through woodland. Eventually a single-arched classical bridge built by James Paine comes into view, while beyond the enormous lake stretches away, a dramatic contrast to the enclosed stream-side path. Eventually a false bridge built by Brown on the far side is revealed as the terminating feature.

His most spectacular and famous creation, however, is at Blenheim, where Vanbrugh's monumental bridge once spanned an open valley and a tiny, undersized canal linking two ponds. By damming the river Glynde Brown raised the water level by fifteen feet, bringing it up exactly to the level at which the bridge's central arch began, and filled the valley with the lake which gave the design its overall unity.

Brown's prodigious output represented the mainstream of fashionable gardening taste in the second half of the eighteenth century; it was a fashion which was widely followed. In each case the creation of a lake, usually as the focal point of the landscape viewed from the house and in a position to afford complementary views back, was almost obligatory.

The most successful landscape designs by the group of men emulating his work all incorporated water. A prime example is Richard Woods' design for Brocket Hall, where one end of the lake is crossed by a three-arched bridge by Paine.

At Kedleston in Derbyshire, where the architect Robert Adam redesigned the landscape as well as completing the house, the transformation was on a scale similar to many of Brown's projects. In addition to removing a road and village from one side of the house and resiting them at a convenient distance, Adam dammed the existing small stream with six weirs to form a lake of nearly thirty acres. His remarks while waiting for the water to rise in the desired manner illustrates the problems of such work: 'It is one of those things one trembles for till proved, as hardly one hundred years experience could convey a just idea of the effects in works of that nature.' The view over the lake from the house was completed with the addition of a three-arched bridge covering one of the weirs, which was further disguised with a cascade.

English Influence

In 1770 Horace Walpole wrote from France, 'English gardening gains ground here prodigiously', and it was to continue to do so throughout the continent well into the nineteenth century in the form of the *jardin anglais*, *giardino inglese* or *Englischer Garten*. The inspiration for such creations often came from direct contact with native English gardens, as in the case of the Marquis de Girardin who, during the 1770s, created at Ermenonville one of the most atmospheric *jardins anglais*. It acquired immediate fame as the burial place of Rousseau, who died in 1778.

Girardin had studied many of the best contemporary gardens during a visit to England and a memorial at Ermenonville acknowledges the influence of William Shenstone's garden at the Leasowens. The Ile des Peupliers, on which Rousseau's tomb stands, is sited in the large lake which Girardin created by damming the water source. In the simple conjunction of slender trees and the surrounding expanse of water, this is perhaps the most successful combination of the 'natural' style and French formality. Elsewhere in France the *jardin anglais* was added to some of the great classical gardens without intruding on the earlier designs, as at Chantilly and Versailles. In these cases the deliberately natural water features were by necessity on a relatively small scale and usually consisted of winding streams through woodland, as in the *jardin anglais* at Chantilly leading to the Hameau, and at Marie Antoinette's Petit Trianon at Versailles.

In France, though, the Landscape style was always viewed by many with disapproval. The informality and picturesque qualities of the style, however, were ideally suited to the mood of German and Central

A lithograph of Ermenonville; the English-inspired landscape style and the presence of Rousseau's tomb on the Ile des Peupliers created an especially interesting and culturally charged environment.

European romanticism. English-style gardens, then, appeared throughout the German states, Czechoslovakia, Hungary and Poland. In some cases, notably the Hungarian gardens of Tata and Martonvasar and Lednice-Valtice in Czechoslovakia, enormous lakes formed the central features of informal landscapes of wood and parkland, enlivened with romantically styled buildings. On the lake at Lednice, which covers some eighty-five acres, are a quantity of small wooded islands, while at Tata the similarly proportioned lake was created by draining an area of marsh; the landscape of nearly six hundred acres was then laid out around the lake.

On a far smaller scale was the Polish garden of Arkadia whose layout and allegorical features are comparable to those of Stourhead. The garden was created by the anglophile Neoclassical architect Szymon Bogumil for Helena Radziwill between 1775 and 1785. Extending to nearly forty acres, it focuses upon a small irregular lake with an island at one end, inspired by the Ile des Peupliers at Ermenonville. Around the lake paths wind through woodland, giving changing views over the water, leading to the various architectural features which overlook it, such as the porticoed Temple of Venus and a semi-circular amphitheatre.

One of the most successful English style Picturesque parks was made at Wilhelmshöhe (opposite) at the beginning of the nineteenth century. The influence spread throughout most of Europe and produced outstanding landscapes at Wörlitz in Germany (above right) and Muskau in Poland (right), where a romantic tower stands surrounded by trees and reflected in the water of the lake.

The landscape created for Catherine the Great at Tsarskoe Selo (above and opposite) was 'natural' in style, incorporating a large lake with islands and a winding stream, and decorated with an array of buildings and other architectural features, including a Palladian bridge and the Chinese temple seen here and on the lower left of the chart opposite.

Another important water feature in the park is the stream which winds along one boundary until it flows away beneath a bridge.

Wörlitz, the earliest landscape park to be made in Germany and also one of the most ambitious, was the result of two extensive tours of English gardens made by Prince Franz of Anhalt-Dessau, accompanied by his architect and team of gardeners. Although clearly inspired by the gardens that he saw – such as Stowe, Stourhead and the Leasowens – the Prince's creation at Wörlitz gave the English style a local interpretation and adopted it to the flat site along the banks of the Elbe. Covering an area of well over one hundred acres and blending into surrounding farmland, the park is largely designed around lakes and a system of waterways which enhance the allegorical significance of the various buildings and other features.

There were considerable technical problems in laying out the park: the waters of the Elbe had to be controlled, while severe flooding in 1770, when the river broke its banks, meant that the project had to be virtually restarted. In 1778 Goethe visited the park and pronounced his seal of approval, 'Here it is now infinitely beautiful. It moved me very much yesterday evening, as we crept through lakes, canals and woods, how the gods had allowed the prince to create a dream around himself. As one passes through it, it is as if one were being told a fairy tale, and has all the character of the Elysian Fields.'

Among the late eighteenth-century rulers of Europe there was none more anglophile than Catherine the Great of Russia. She made clear her admiration for English gardens in enthusiastic tones in a letter to Voltaire written in 1772, 'I now love to distraction gardens in the English style, the curving lines, the gentle slopes, the ponds in the form of lakes, the archipelagos on dry land, and I scorn straight lines and twin allées. I hate fountains which torture water in order to make it follow a course contrary to its nature ... in a word anglomania rules my plantomania.' Her reign, which witnessed Russia's rise to a position of primacy in continental Europe, greatly benefited the landowning aristocracy, who then began to take an increased interest in their estates. This, and the fashionable cultural romanticism, ensured that the English landscape style was widely applied up to the time of the Napoleonic invasion.

Catherine's most important garden was at Tsarskoe Selo outside St. Petersburg, where the Empress Elizabeth had built the first of two palaces (the second was added in the early nineteenth century by Alexander I). Her architect Vasily Neelov had visited England, while the existing formal garden was replanned by John Busch, an Englishman

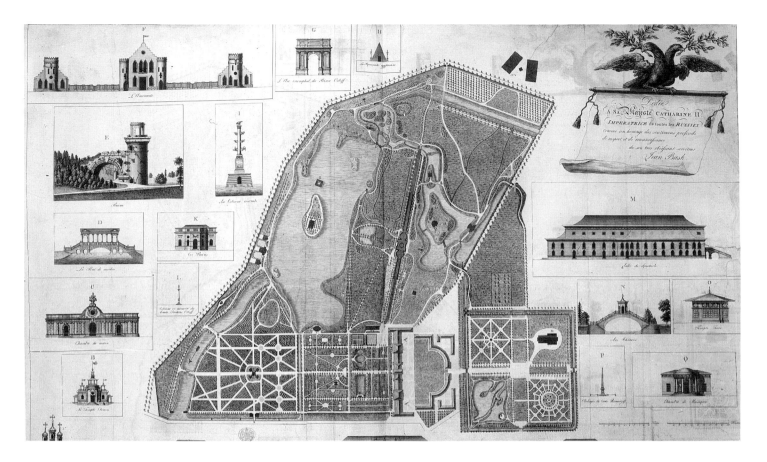

whom she had brought to Russia. The main alteration was the naturalization of a rectangular basin into a large lake, at one end of which Neelov built a Palladian bridge in the style of those at Stowe and Wilton. The impressive Baroque grotto built earlier by Bartolomeo Rastrelli, which overlooked the lake, was retained, while winding streams were introduced throughout the newly made parkland. In one area these formed part of a Chinese garden with buildings by the Scottish architect, Charles Cameron.

At roughly the same time as Catherine was creating the landscape at Tsarskoe Selo, her son, Grand Duke Paul, and his German wife were creating a garden a few miles away at Pavlovsk, beside the river Slavyanka. Charles Cameron was also employed here, adding many buildings, notably the rotunda called the Temple of Friendship which stands beside a stream winding through woodland. The imperial example was taken up by the Russian aristocracy in the nineteenth century, the predominant style being woodland and water landscapes laid out around the various country seats close to St. Petersburg.

Water and Landscape Architecture

By the late eighteenth century and early nineteenth the Landscape style had become fashionable in the private gardens of royalty and aristocracy all over Europe. As the nineteenth century developed, however, it was also to become the favoured style of the new urban public parks, both in Europe and the United States. In Munich, the Englischer Garten was begun in 1789 on the orders of Elector Karl Theodor and was to expand to an eventual size of some 900 acres. Much of the design was carried out early in the nineteenth century by Friedrich Ludwig Sckell, who had previously landscaped parts of the garden at Schwetzingen, incorporating a network of small streams and the main lake, originally close to one side until the park was substantially extended. The Englischer Garten was particularly important because, without an architectural focal point, it was given shape and structure by its system of water features. It was also effectively created from nothing, in contrast, for instance, to the transformation of the Bois de Boulogne on the edge of Paris, carried out under Napoléon III. The formal *ronds-points* at the junctions of long straight *allées* were replaced by two sinuous lakes covering a much larger area. This made the role of water far more substantial than had originally been the case in the old, predominantly forested design.

In England the most influential public park was Birkenhead Park near Liverpool, laid out by Joseph Paxton between 1843–47. The site's marshy ground and the need for the park to be self-sufficient in views and attractive features combined to confirm Paxton's original conviction that the major features should be two lakes. Positioned towards the two sides of the park, both lakes had sinuous inlets and headlands, as well as an island which added to their naturalistic appearance. His plan was an unqualified success. The lakes, disguised from many angles by artificial mounds of earth with planting, added an element of surprise and seclusion to the park's generally open appearance. They also provided the possibility of recreation – boating – and rural qualities, an important factor in the provision of relief from the urban environment.

Birkenhead became the model for the public parks that appeared in most major British cities in the second half of the nineteenth century, although few, if any, competed in quality. Perhaps more significant was the inspiration, on both social and landscape design levels, which Birkenhead proved to the American, Frederick Law Olmsted, when he visited England in 1850. Olmsted returned to the United States and

This Victorian engraving of Paxton's innovative Birkenhead Park, Lancashire (above) shows one of his boat houses, while the photograph shows a view of the lake today (opposite).

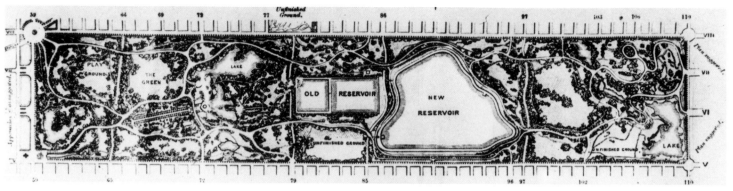

A combination of winding lakes and streams was fundamental to the structure of all Frederick Law Olmsted's urban park plans, including Central Park, New York (above) and Back Bay, Boston (opposite).

devoted the majority of the rest of his career to public landscape work; by the end of the century, thanks to him, America's public parks enjoyed an unrivalled position throughout the world.

His first project was New York's Central Park, begun in 1857, against considerable odds, both administrative and in terms of the terrain. Although the design is obviously different to Birkenhead, Olmsted appreciated that Central Park, also enclosed by urban development, had to be similarly self-sufficient in offering enjoyable, visually attractive features. And it was the water features, especially the large new reservoir, as the main lake was originally called, which were to play a crucial role.

Olmsted's later parks were, in the main, laid out free of the constrictions that surrounded Central Park and as a result show far more design freedom. At Brooklyn's Prospect Park, the major expanse of the lake dominates one side of the park and from here the water winds through, passing beneath driveway and foot bridges and gently decreasing in size without losing the natural irregularity along its banks.

It was in Boston, however, that Olmsted arguably created his greatest system of parks, which became integral to the city's whole character and appearance, not least because of the original watery nature of their sites. These included the boggy ground of Back Bay and the site of Jamaica Park, dominated by water in lakes, winding creeks and streams.

With the decrease in the scale of the average private garden throughout the nineteenth century and, to some degree, changes in taste, public parks such as those laid out by Olmsted increasingly became the primary outlets for major landscaping, both in the United States and Europe. While the aspirations of the designers of such parks were quite different from the creators of the private gardens of eighteenth-century England, they continued to demonstrate similar concerns about the incorporation of water in large-scale landscaping.

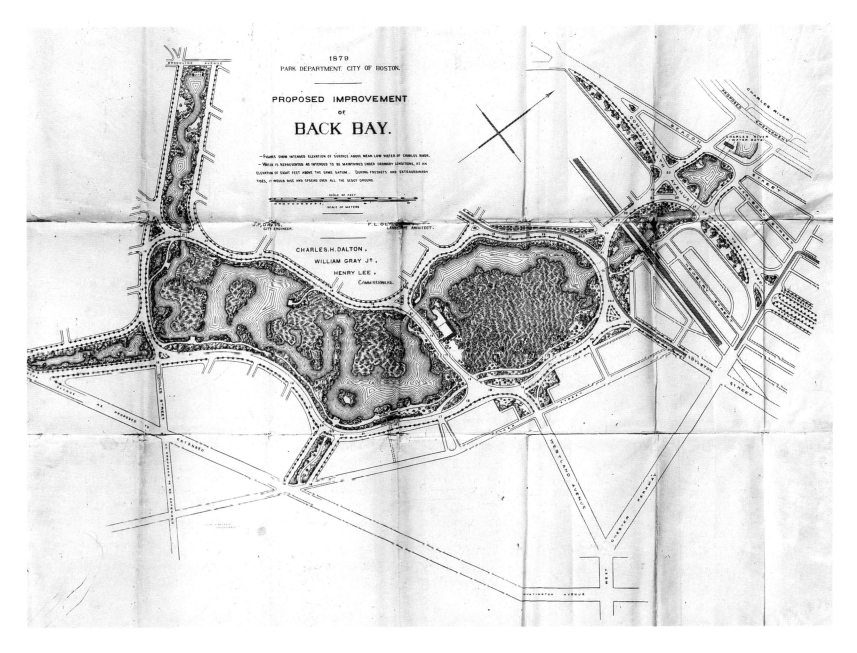

1879

PARK DEPARTMENT. CITY OF BOSTON.

PROPOSED IMPROVEMENT
OF
BACK BAY.

Throughout the twentieth century the emerging profession of
landscape architect has had to take account of a number of primary
influences: its roots in garden design; its relationship with architecture;
its role in town planning and the creation of urban landscapes; its need to
allow for extensive public access; and its environmental impact and
relationship with the natural landscape. The integration of water has
often proved to be of decisive importance in the shaping of a scheme,

Geoffrey Jellicoe's imaginative roof-top water garden gave a new dimension to Harvey's store, Guildford, providing relief to shoppers who had progressed through the trading floors.

both in terms of original design and the impact and quality of the completed landscape. For some designers, water has provided the most acceptable means of continuity with the past traditions of classical garden design, while for others it has provided the means of creating a landscape which has no requirement for historical precedent. The work of Roberto Burle Marx in Brasilia has demonstrated emphatically how water can be combined successfully with the harsh lines of Modernist architecture, providing visual and textural contrast.

In many instances, the water features of landscape architecture are undoubtedly of greater interest than those of the contemporary private garden, not least because the work has been carried out often for munificent and enlightened clients who wish to create a landscape of real originality. Such projects have varied from public parks extending to hundreds of acres to the atriums of modern office blocks planned around a cascading waterfall. Of course, such quality is not always evident; there are few more depressing pictures that a grey concrete office block reflected mournfully in a badly-built and proportioned pool surrounded by uninteresting, convenience planting. But there is no question that – certainly in the last few decades – the potential for interesting large-scale water landscapes has been in the realm of landscape architecture and no longer in the average private garden.

In much contemporary landscape architecture community participation has been a high priority and many of the most successful designs have been created in response to this. Water is spectacular and it is also fun, as demonstrated in the numerous intricate and ebullient fountains built on many public sites. It also provides recreational opportunities whether for boating, fishing or swimming and, not the least consideration in many instances, a lake, fountain or cascade is low on maintenance costs once created.

Two designs by Geoffrey Jellicoe, one a department store roof garden and the other a lake in a new town development, both created during the 1950s, when the idealism of landscape architecture was at a high point, illustrate in markedly different ways the successful use of water as a primary feature. At Harvey's store in Guildford, Jellicoe created a rooftop fantasy which, while technically following the famous pre-war example of Derry and Toms in Kensington, set out more deliberately to provide an environment that would challenge human sensations. The impact of the water garden on the roof is undoubtedly made much more powerful for the shopper by the ascent through the more mundane levels of the store's sales floors.

Jellicoe himself has written very evocatively on the garden: 'Upon emerging from the security of the shop below you are confronted with the prospect of a hazardous venture. Dare you go forth into this wild sky garden and complete the circuit with all its excitements and dangers? . . . Here is the test of courage: a river that flows into the sky and is crossed only by stepping stones that are unreal because they float off the water. Will they sink under your weight or carry you off to the edge of eternity . . . At Harvey's there is the sensation of adventure and peril, of surprise and the unexpected, of pleasure in accomplishment, of the feel of wet and dry, and above all the modified excitement of being part of an environment that is removed from the every day and is faintly heroic, like the abode of the gods . . .'

The extensive water garden created by Geoffrey Jellicoe out of a small stream at Hemel Hempstead brought a softening, natural element into his plan for the town (above left *and* above).

Quite different are the creative aims and final appearance of the water garden at Hemel Hempstead new town. This is a narrow strip between the main town and its car parks, through which flowed a small and uninteresting stream and which had to be open to public access. Damming, excavation and the landscaping of the spoil into mounded banks transformed the stream into an elegant canal flowing into a lake with a fountain jet and crossed by interestingly positioned bridges. This water garden linked together seemingly disjointed and ugly areas and provided the new town with an elegant landscape feature.

The presence of water on a planned site has an immediate effect upon related buildings. Looking, for instance, at the settings created by Roberto Burle Marx for the various impressive but nonetheless stark and

uncompromising Modernist government buildings in Brasilia, it would be hard to imagine them without the intricate and expansive pools, canals, fountains and cascades which are the structural linchpins of his landscape designs. It has been the same situation in landscape architecture projects all over the world, especially where the building elements are sited in an environment of predominantly hard landscape.

This has certainly been true for the landscape architects of Thomas Church's Californian school, whose work has spread through many of the major cities of the United States. In Fountain Plaza, Dallas, Dan Kiley created a total water landscape of fountains and descending cascades which mixes formality and freer elements which are a recreation of the natural scenery of North America's native rivers. Another admired creation of the Californian school is Lawrence Halprin's Lovejoy Fountain Plaza in Portland, Oregon, where the designer appeals directly to human emotion in a dramatic cascade of water which swirls around steps between large, geometrical pools. Halprin employed similar techniques in his design of the Seattle Freeway Park where the major priority was to integrate the noisy and potentially intrusive road system into the surrounding landscape.

Roberto Burle Marx designed this garden for the Hospital Da Lagoa, Rio de Janeiro; the Marx style is characterized by the juxtaposition of dramatic tropical planting and Modernist architecture.

The use of water to bring vigorous movement to modern landscape architecture is exemplified in Lawrence Halprin's Lovejoy Fountain Plaza, Portland, Oregon (right) and Dan Kiley's Fountain Plaza, Dallas, Texas (opposite).

Stream and Pond Gardens

*P*ond and stream designs, both formal and natural, are a notable feature of the twentieth-century garden. Planting around the edges of the water and aquatic plants on its surface may be used to soften the lines of a formal pool (above) and to enhance the 'natural' aspects of a more relaxed design (opposite).

Aᴌᴛʜᴏᴜɢʜ the elevation of total design above the traditional opposition of formal and informal had been the aim of many Modernist landscape designers, in the great majority of Western gardens tradition and taste have usually ensured that the contrast has been retained. Indeed, the two have often been juxtaposed in a garden to give variety and a sense of progression from orderliness to a more natural scene. At Shute House, Jellicoe's garden derives its distinctive character from the varied treatment of water in the woodland pools, the canal and the descending rill. Similar contrasts in the various water features have been created to great effect in other gardens; at Abbotswood, for instance, a stream garden has been created on sloping ground beyond the terraces around the house. From a garden of water and architecture, it gradually becomes one of water and plants, positioned on either bank through woodland and open meadow.

In two gardens, Cornwell Manor, Gloucestershire, and Abbots Ripton Hall, Cambridgeshire, the contrasting treatment of water is achieved along the course of a single stream. The former is the work of Clough Williams-Ellis, carried out in the late 1930s and designed to harmonize with the elegant late seventeenth-century façade of the house and the sloping lawn which descends to the stream flowing across the foot of the garden. From the entry of the water into the garden, Williams-Ellis channelled it into a narrow stone-edged canal; this then widens into a circular pool on the central axis, while the house provides the ideal central point of a vista down the lawn and up the steep incline on the other side, where stone steps lead to wrought-iron gates. The canal's formality is further emphasized by pairs of yews and weeping pear trees aligned on either side. Where the formal canal ends the water returns to a more natural state, descending through two successive rock gardens and a bog garden, before flowing into a series of three lakes out of sight in the valley below.

The garden at Abbots Ripton is more recent, having been created since the 1960s by the house's owner, Lord de Ramsay, with assistance from the architect Peter Foster. While there is much else of interest, one of the main features is the Abbots Ripton brook which flows into the garden beneath the boundary wall on one side and parallel to one side of the house. Where the water enters the garden Peter Foster has built a small bridge with Doric columns and a grotto against the boundary wall.

*At Cornwell Manor, Oxfordshire, the pool (*above*) is the centre-piece of the formalized section of water designed by Clough Williams-Ellis and makes a dramatic foreground to the view up to the house beyond. At Abbots Ripton, Cambridgeshire, a natural stream has been canalized to make a semi-formal stretch of water embellished with a 'Chinese Chippendale' bridge (*opposite*).*

From here, the stream is canalized to flow along the lawn's edge to a small island rockery which has three fountain jets positioned on the axis of the house and a long vista between double herbaceous borders on the far side. From the fountain the water flows beneath a white-painted wooden Chinese Chippendale bridge, beyond which it reverts to its natural state, winding beneath a large plane tree and on past shrubberies and meadow grass to where a rustic octagonal summer-house confirms the water's change of mood. On the garden's edge the brook flows beneath an eighteenth-century three-arched brick bridge and on to the garden's most impressive landscape feature, a five-acre lake whose visual attraction is greatly enhanced by the Chinese fishing pavilion built by Peter Foster as an eye-catcher at the far end. The real purpose of the lake, however, is practical – to irrigate the surrounding farmland.

As many stream and pond gardens demonstrate, an ideal planting combination is provided by select numbers of waterside plants in bold groups in conjunction with trees such as birches, maples and live oaks, planted individually or in small groups in the areas on either side of the water. This type of planting is equally suitable for streams and informal ponds. In such cases a sensitive handling of scale is vital: a long bank of deciduous azaleas or a similar flowering shrub may be impressive along the far side of a large pond or lake, but would be overpowering if the area of water is too small. In the case of smaller pools colour would be more suitably provided by primulas, for instance.

As one might imagine, the doyenne of twentieth-century gardeners, Gertrude Jekyll, had detailed opinions on water gardens and wrote in 1901 about her ideal stream garden in terms which remain relevant today: 'I should be careful not to crowd too many different plants into my stream-picture. Where the Forget-me-nots are it would be quite enough to see them and the double Meadow-Sweet, and some good hardy moisture-loving Fern, Osmunda or Lady Fern ... Close by the stream-side and quite out of view of other flowering plants should be a bold planting of *Iris lavigata*, the handsome Japanese kind, perhaps better known as *Iris kaempferi* ... The yellow Mumulus (*M. luteus*) is a capital thing for the stream-side; once planted it will take care of itself; indeed it has become naturalized by many streams in England. ...

'It should be noted that in such a stream-garden it will usually be the opposite side that is best seen, and this should be borne in mind while composing the pictures and setting out the path ... As the stream leads further away we begin to forget the garden, and incline towards a wish for the beautiful things of our own wilds, so that here would be, for the

Rhododendrons and other flowering shrubs give colour and excitement to natural woodland around this descending series of lakes and streams at Hodnet Hall, Shropshire.

earliest water flowers of the year, the smaller of the wild kinds of Water Buttercup ... After this the character of the stream shows a change for here is a clump of Alders ... Now is the time to make some important effect with plants of a larger size, that will prepare the eye, as it were, for the larger scale of the water-loving trees.'

At Hodnet Hall, Shropshire, the water garden created between the First and Second World Wars and steadily embellished since is on a scale which can be matched by very few others. Admiring the garden today, it is hard to imagine that the vista of descending lakes and ponds linked by streams, whose size and flow is constantly changing, was partly man-made. The building of dams caused the flooding of naturally boggy ground, creating, notably, the main lake beyond the ground which slopes down from the house's south front. Around this large expanse of water the planting is suitably bold, with large clumps of moisture-loving plants along the edges and banks of flowering shrubs set back and extending into natural woodland. The wooded surroundings of much of the water garden gives it a vital element of secrecy and enables the atmosphere to become progressively more natural away from the central areas of the garden. This is especially noticeable in a succession of three ponds which lead in one direction towards the garden's boundary and larger lakes beyond and which are partly shrouded on both banks by native woodland underplanted with selected smaller flowering trees and shrubs. Below the main lake, where some of the smaller ponds are more open, the waterside planting is more dense, with combinations of flower and foliage provided by lush gunnera and lysichitons and more delicate astilbes or candelabra primulas.

The water garden at Hodnet is entirely in character with the natural wooded valleys of the Shropshire countryside. Similarly, the ten-acre garden at Longstock, Hampshire, is ideally suited to the setting of the gently moving chalk streams which provide its source. The garden has been created over the last forty years and provides a very good example of how water can be effectively distributed through a large area, but with minimal descent and flow. The water comes from the river Test and from where it enters the garden at the top it is directed through three, almost imperceptibly differentiated levels by a system of sluices. In all, it falls only three feet before flowing away to be channelled back into the main stream. The water then flows through a system of streams and lagoons – where its gentle movement allows great spreads of white and pink water-lilies to flourish – all with curving edges and encircling a number of small islands. Everywhere, the banks are planted with large groups of single

Copious and luxuriant planting envelops the water garden at Longstock Hall, Hampshire, where the water flows over a series of shallow sluices (centre left); a thatched summer-house (top left) adds a rustic air. At the Old Rectory, Burghfield, Berkshire (lower left), the figure of Antinous rising from the water demonstrates the dramatic effect of statuary in water.

173

*The garden of Brook Cottage, Oxford
(above) is notable for the profusion and
variety of its planting, which is given focus
by the placing of a pond near the centre of
the garden. Monet's garden (opposite) at
Giverny is essentially a pond garden
made by the damming of a passing stream.
Its creation was a revolution in garden
design in that it shifted attention away
from water as an accompaniment to
architecture to the concept that water and
planting together could form highly
attractive garden designs with minimal
additions, such as a Japanese-style bridge.*

plants which flower progressively through the year; these include
primulas, astilbes and lobelias, with many varieties of hosta prominent
among the foliage plants. One of the garden's most striking features
comes in winter with the brilliant red, orange and yellow young stems of
pollarded willows; in the autumn the shape and foliage of individual trees
like the swamp cypress and liquidambar are made doubly impressive by
their reflections.

A quite different effect and scale to those of gardens such as Hodnet
or Longstock, where the whole character of the garden revolves around
the progress of water, is achieved where smaller ponds exist in gardens
dominated by areas of rich planting. In such cases the presence of water
acts as a foil to the planted areas but may also be a force for continuity
when the planting is extended along its edges. This is the case at the Old
Rectory garden in Berkshire where impressive herbaceous borders
backed by yew hedges lead away from the house towards the contrasting
area of a natural pond, encircled by a grass path backed by dense,
progressively heightening planting. A stone statue of Antinous set on a
low plinth in the centre of the water looks back up the borders and
provides the link between natural and formal. Similarly, at Brook
Cottage, Oxfordshire, the small pond near the centre of the garden makes
an interesting feature which, at the same time, harmonizes with the
garden's rich planting which encircles the water and includes hostas,
euphorbias and iris.

The suitability of more or less 'natural' ponds and streams as sites has
proved a marvellous opportunity to exploit that twentieth-century taste
for a combination of horticulture and natural vegetation to express itself.
Whether on the scale of an enchanted woodland setting or something on
a far more modest scale, some very satisfying results have been achieved
through the balancing of the two elements. Some such schemes have
been created as individual features and some as part of an overall garden
design. In the latter, they have often provided the perfect way to
complete the sense of progression from formal areas around a house to
increasing naturalness towards the perimeter, as advocated by Gertrude
Jekyll at the beginning of the century and sought by gardeners ever since.
Even compared to the style of formal water in the modern garden, such
stream and pond gardens with colourful waterside planting are an almost
exclusively twentieth-century creation and, as such, one of the most
significant aspects of the period's contribution to the creative use of
water in the garden.

A comparable desire for communion with nature inspired the painter

A view from a bridge at Giverny (above) *shows the delightful combination of extensive planting and larger stretches of water. Equally interesting, but on a smaller scale, are the 'harmonic' waterfalls* (opposite) *introduced by Geoffrey Jellicoe at Shute House, Wiltshire, which rely for their full effect on the contrast between their different musical pitches.*

Claude Monet during the 1890s to create a pond in his garden at Giverny; this was to become the most important single subject in his painting for the rest of his career. Created by diverting water from a passing stream, the pond was enclosed with willows, planted with water-lilies and embellished with a Japanese-style wooden bridge. It provided the artist with a simple but constantly changing environment of water, colour and light. The creation of this garden also marked the shift from the role of water in the garden being predominantly architectural to being at least equally plant related, a tendency which was to gather pace through the twentieth century.

Affinity with natural surroundings was to become the most important single thread in the modern American garden once the fashion for the Beaux-Arts style had passed. This concern proved equally relevant to Modernist gardens on the edge of the Californian desert or in the woodlands of New England or Massachusetts. In many such gardens it was water and its related features which provided the unifying link. The ideal produced one of the most celebrated of American domestic landscape creations in 1936 when Frank Lloyd Wright designed a house called 'Falling Water' in Pennsylvania for his visionary client Edgar J. Kaufman. The site's inspiration was a waterfall and Wright designed the house to perch over the water and blend with its surroundings, as he noted himself: 'There in a beautiful forest was a solid high rock-edge beside a waterfall and the natural thing seemed to be to cantilever the house from that rock bank over the falling water . . . I think you can hear the waterfall when you look at the design.'

Perhaps the most essential development in the twentieth-century water garden has been the breakdown of the traditional differentiation of formal and informal styles. Frank Lloyd Wright's 'Falling Water' demonstrated how modern architecture could be combined with natural surroundings in a way which was to be taken up by landscape architects throughout the century, often in large-scale public or civic designs. As the quantity of gardens has grown, though, the average scale and size has decreased, so modern materials and techniques – plastics and the electric pump, for instance – have facilitated the introduction of water into gardens on a small, domestic scale. While the flamboyance or vast extent of the famous water creations of past periods may be beyond the means of the modern gardener, the effect of contemporary water features remains the same.

The natural attractions of flowing water
can be enhanced dramatically by the
addition of waterfalls. They were much
favoured by the garden designers of the
Landscape Movement in the eighteenth
century, as at Wilhelmshöhe (top). They
recognized that rapidly moving water, even
when theatrical and contrived, always
evokes the impression of a natural,
untutored landscape. During the twentieth
century waterfalls have returned to favour
in the context of stream gardens, as in
these examples: Kildrummy Castle,
Scotland (opposite), Finlaystone House,
Scotland (above) and Abbotswood,
Gloucestershire (right).

The water-lily, or nymphaea, *is the most enduring of aquatic plants, its beauty stemming from the carpet effect of foliage on the surface of water.*

Aquatic plants divide into two distinct categories: those that actually grow in the water, and those that thrive in the damp conditions along the water's edge. One, however, has dominated the relationship between plants and water throughout gardening history and all over the world – the lotus, water-lily or *nymphaea* and the related *nelumbo* of China. White water-lilies were of religious importance in the earliest Egyptian gardens and usually the only aquatic plants grown. Indeed, similar plants of one kind or another have been portrayed as having symbolic importance in most of the religions of the world. For many centuries, though, planting in water was common only in Oriental or Islamic gardens; in Western gardens water was traditionally incorporated more as an architectural feature devoid of any planting.

Today, the water-lily, including hardy and tropical varieties, is grown throughout the world for the combination of its cup-like flowers, which range from deep red to pink, yellow and white, and their floating, luxuriant leaves. Many of the most successful aquatic or damp-loving plants owe their popularity to such a combined effect of flower and foliage: for instance, in temperate regions certain primulas, irises and astilbes, all of which thrive along the water's edge. In a garden pool with little or no flow of water, plants play an important role in maintaining the supply of oxygen, limiting algae and, if necessary, providing shelter and food for fish. Trees and shrubs suitable for growing in damp conditions include some with outstanding foliage such as the deciduous conifer *Taxodium disticum* (swamp cypress), which is the most prevalent natural tree in the Florida Everglades, and the *nyssas* and others of elegant, sinuous shape such as poplars, birches and willows.

Aquatic Plants

The numerous varieties of the water-lily are illustrated here by Nymphaea m. *'Rosea' (*above left)*,* Nymphaea m. *'Chromatella' (*above centre) *and* Nymphaea m.japonica *(*above right)*.

EVER SINCE *the time of Pompeii and Herculaneum, water has been used in small gardens to transform visual appearance and mood; judging the correct scale for the features is of crucial importance. Where space is at a premium, the individual elements of a garden gain significance and considerable thought has to be given to their size and prominence. In more expansive gardens, where perhaps there is the added attraction of surrounding countryside and spectacular views, the various features can be enjoyed in a relatively leisurely way. In the smallest town gardens, however, there may easily be only one view, revealed at once. In such gardens the addition of a suitable water feature can have a dramatic impact on the garden's presence and style.*

A*stilbes, lysitichums and ferns are highlights in this medley of waterside plants.*

Features of the Small Water Garden

A cistern at La Pietra, Italy.

Cistern

Cisterns have been used to collect and store water in gardens from earliest times and were widely used in Roman gardens. Traditionally made of lead or iron from the Renaissance onwards in Europe, they were often highly decorated with classical reliefs, coats-of-arms, crests, initials or dates. Occasionally they were positioned against a house at the foot of a downpipe to collect rain-water. They have become extremely popular as ornamental features in contemporary gardens, either for their original purpose of holding water, or to contain plants. They make a particularly interesting water feature in the small garden.

Dipping-well

As an architectural water feature, the dipping-well has considerable potential for small gardens. Usually set against a retaining or boundary wall, the well consists of a small basin or pool, possibly raised, above which the wall contains a vaulted arch which partially covers the basin, and from which water is fed by a wall mask or fountain. Such a feature can either be self-contained or allow for the water to overflow the basin and feed into other architectural features. Wells were widely used in Italian Renaissance gardens where they were ideal features for gardens with terracing and retaining walls. The dipping-well was also one of Lutyens' favourite architectural water features.

A dipping-well at Hestercombe, Somerset, designed by Sir Edwin Lutyens.

Font

Stone fonts for baptismal water have recently begun to be re-used in small contemporary gardens as ornamental features, either with or without water.

Trough

A simple container, usually of stone, such as a trough, can be usefully employed to introduce water into gardens of limited size.

Well and Well-head

Wells have often been the only available supply of water for gardens in dry climates and in some instances gardens have been sited and laid out over a well, incorporated either by feeding into a fountain or directly into a pool or basin. Originally the well-head was a simple stone structure covering the well and sometimes carrying a wheel for lowering and raising a bucket. They later became far more decorative, notably in Italy, and in the contemporary garden they have often been re-used as ornamental features in their own right.

A well-head at Iford Manor Gardens, Wiltshire.

The Small Water Garden

7

Small gardens often closely reflect local cultural traditions. The gardens of modern-day Spanish cities, especially the Moorish-Andalusian ones of Cordoba, Seville and Granada, are deeply rooted in the Islamic courtyard garden that was perfected in its essentials hundreds of years ago. Water, in a small formal pool, is almost invariably the most popular central feature, ideally with a bubble fountain or low fountain jet. The atmosphere of these gardens is architectural; the courtyards are paved, plants or citrus trees are in terracotta or stone pots and there are often low walls; the splashing water, bright colours and strong scent of the favoured plants give them a cheerful, animated atmosphere. Such an arrangement can be successful on the smallest possible scale and is ideally suited to a region where warm sunlight is plentiful.

Similar national cultural tendencies can be seen in small English-style gardens, both urban and rural where the recreation of the atmosphere of the countryside has remained a strong tradition.

There are numerous urban gardens where the focal point is a natural pond, although this may be reduced by necessity to an area of a few square feet. Despite the possibility of reduced scale, however, screening with trees or shrubs to hide the water from the rest of the garden, and selective planting of the same moisture-loving plants which commonly adorn far larger pond and stream gardens, can create the desired effect of luxuriant informality. Because of the added possibility of incorporating views over surrounding countryside, small rural gardens often have greater potential than those in towns and cities; several water feature elements – landscape, natural and formal – can be successfully juxtaposed within a small area. A small water garden is often most successful when it is enclosed and secretive, with paths winding between a plethora of naturalized plants; the dramatic effect of the planting can be heightened if, for instance, there is a window in the tree canopy to a stretch of natural water beyond. Other natural features, such as old ponds, can be transformed by planting a variety of predominantly foliage plants around its edges and incorporated into a garden beside more formal elements, such as a small fountain or rectangular pool.

Small spaces are brought alive by the addition of statuary to water features.

Many Spanish gardens in the Moorish/Andalusian tradition (opposite) display a small-scale perfection within courtyard confines. Architecture and planting are given life and interest by the sight and sound of water in motion.

The spouts and fountains illustrated here show how formal water features can be scaled down to fit in with the compressed vistas offered by the small garden. Had any of these spouts or jets been larger, then the features may very well have seemed inappropriately grand for these limited and highly architectural spaces. As it is, their small-scale sculptural details effectively add layers of meaning to their respective gardens.

*S*mall gardens or even small enclosed areas within larger gardens are rendered infinitely more interesting by the presence of pools, formal and informal. The reflective qualities of water, especially, add unexpected dimensions to the smallest place, as witness the repeated image of the sculpture wall by Ben Nicholson at Sutton Place (below right), or the reflection of statuary in the pool (below left).

This double wooden seat is placed ingeniously across a stream at Shute House, Wiltshire.

Rural gardens, obviously, have the potential advantage of a relationship with the surrounding landscape, while the small urban garden usually has to exist within rigidly geometric boundaries and needs to be entirely self-sufficient. As a result, the harmonious integration of its component parts is of crucial importance and nothing demonstrates this better than the use of water features. In many gardens the installation of a fountain may seem an attractive idea but, once in position, it may fail to harmonize with the rest of the garden or to become the main focal point it was originally intended to be. This may be because the style or scale of the piece – perhaps surmounted with an unsuitable figure – is wrong, or because a small single jet of water looks out of place. If the sound of moving water is desired in a confined area a more effective solution is often provided by a wall mask, or *mascaron*, spouting water into a basin, or by a raised basin fed at one point by a miniature cascade. Both are intrinsically small-scale features – rather than large ones reduced down – and have the advantage of being set against a wall and therefore of providing a focal point, an illusion of increased scale in a small, enclosed garden. If a raised basin is installed, the size of the cascade feeding it should be determined using the principles of the Japanese garden: that small is beautiful and two or three stones or boulders are quite sufficient to achieve the desired effect.

Possibly the most important attraction of water in this context is its ability to add an extra dimension to a small garden, whatever its style. This may be a horticultural setting, with lush planting, or a modern design of predominantly hard features, which is often the most practical solution for a severely restricted area where low maintenance costs have to be combined with the demands of contemporary living. The shape of simple pools can be chosen to match their surroundings; however hard the material used – wood decking, stone or brick – the area of water will integrate with the overall design of the garden in a way, for instance, that detailed planting might not. A number of contemporary garden designers have demonstrated this to great effect in gardens where the available space is extremely limited and the desired effect is one of achieving simple unity between geometric forms. In such cases, the water surface is best left undisturbed so that, as well as blending into the predominantly horizontal planes of the design, reflection adds a vertical element.

Among twentieth-century garden designers Russell Page was one who particularly enjoyed integrating water into his creations of greatly varying size. In most of his gardens water was part of the overall plan and his particular skill was in balancing the size and emphasis of a pool or canal and its related decoration of ornament or planting with the other features of the garden. In some cases, however, water was made the predominant feature, as in the garden of the Frick Museum in New York, which he began in 1973. The site of the garden was a small rectangle enclosed and overlooked on three sides by towering classical buildings and with a gateway giving on to the street on the fourth. Keeping selected planting to the perimeter walls, he filled most of the area with lawn centred upon a rectangular pool. The subtlety of the finished garden is described by Gabrielle van Zuylen: 'Years before, in Holland, Page had noticed how water served to enlarge one's sense of actual distance, and so he employed this optical trick at the Frick, using a third of the lawn to make a rectangular pool flush with the ground and rimmed with flat narrow stone. He filled it with water lilies and American lotus and had a fountain jet installed in the centre to provide interest in winter.'

Water in the garden does play strongly on the sensibility of the beholder and therein lies its universal appeal, which is not always fully recognized. For Geoffrey Jellicoe gardens and landscape are intimately connected to the human subconscious. This recalls the earliest concept of the garden as paradise and central to this concept is water. At Shute House Jellicoe specifically planned the varied treatment of water both to provide and respond to different human moods, but in his later, more ambitious work at Sutton Place he sought to achieve relationships of the utmost simplicity in the garden of the Ben Nicholson wall. Looking at the geometric squares and circles of the massive white marble relief reflected in the formal pool in front, occasionally merging with groups of water-lilies, does evoke a sense of elemental purity.

The garden of the Frick Museum, New York, designed by Russell Page.

Tropical and Oriental Water Gardens

8

THE ABUNDANCE of regular torrential rainfall in most tropical countries has ensured that water has been integral to many tropical gardens, sometimes by necessity, as a response to the need for it to be controlled and collected, and to complement the lush vegetation and vivid flora.

In South-East Asia formal designs created around an abundant source of water characterized some of the earliest tropical gardens, laid out around royal palaces and Hindu and Buddhist temples. Water spouted into canals and pools from fountains decorated with the figures of deities or grotesque animals. The water was often closely integrated with buildings, usually through artistic considerations, but sometimes to overcome a practical problem as in the case of the Buddhist monasteries of Thailand, where the libraries were housed in small pavilions built on stilts over a canal or pool to protect the manuscripts from white ants.

The strong European influences which were assimilated into many tropical countries during the long period of colonial conquest and trading ensured that architectural formality in gardens was perpetuated. The European presence also brought about important changes by introducing botanical gardens to tropical countries, such as the Peradeniya Garden at Kandy, Sri Lanka, established by the British during the 1820s. During this period European gardeners were fascinated by the wealth of exotic plants that grew in tropical countries, a fascination illustrated by the giant water-lily, *Victoria amazonica*, originally named *Victoria regia* after the English queen. This plant, with its great saucer-like leaves and huge flowers, is among the most distinctive features of tropical water gardens. It was so admired by Europeans that it provoked strong competition between gardeners to achieve the first successful flowering in Europe. In England the prize went, perhaps not surprisingly, to the Duke of Devonshire at Chatsworth. At huge expense he commissioned the collection of specimens, while his gardener Joseph Paxton built a special greenhouse with a central tank to contain the plant, which flowered there in 1849. Although the Lily House has gone, *Victoria amazonica* still flowers at Chatsworth in a new greenhouse.

In many gardens in hot climates water often provides the focus for exotic and abundant planting, providing environments of escape from the often oppressive conditions of the tropics, as in the gardens of the Bali Hyatt hotel (opposite and above).

Victoria amazonica, *the giant water-lily, still flowers at Chatsworth, Derbyshire, over 150 years after it was introduced into the garden. It had first flowered there in a special greenhouse built in 1849. It is also illustrated on p. 192.*

During the twentieth century the great plant wealth of tropical countries has been extensively integrated into private gardens and public parks all over the world. The quantity of available water and speed of growth attained by many plants, coupled with lush foliage and brilliant flowers, has given tropical gardens the opportunity to achieve the most spectacular harmony between horticulture and water. The traditional relationship of formal and informal elements is replaced by one of texture, colour and sound. The lushness of vegetation, variety of plants available and speed of growth present a picture in which water is almost indispensable. This was the combination of characteristics which inspired one of the most significant figures of twentieth-century landscape and garden design, the Brazilian Roberto Burle Marx. Inspired by the native plants of his tropical home country, Burle Marx transformed his early career as a painter into garden designer. At a time when Brazil was moving into the vanguard of modern architecture between the wars in São Paolo and, more significantly, from 1960 in the building of the country's new capital city at Brasilia, Burle Marx's work was to prove the ideal foil to much of the new building.

All of Burle Marx's work has been inspired by his love of native Brazilian plants and of the country's dense forests dissected by river systems which he has long fought to preserve. Whether in a small private garden or the far more extensive surroundings of new government buildings in Brasilia, he has worked consistently to combine plant material and water with architecture and abstract sculpture. Free from the limitations imposed by well-entrenched gardening traditions elsewhere in the world, he has been able to respond to the requirements of a particular site in a totally contemporary manner. In his creation of water gardens one of the most remarkable aspects has been the manner in which he has moulded concrete into curving natural shapes to form pools or to define the banks of a stream.

In the settings he has designed for buildings in Brasilia, Burle Marx's use of water acknowledges the importance of man-made structures. At the same time, the water is seen as an opportunity to introduce a natural element into the landscape. At the Ministry of Foreign Affairs, the extensive moat surrounding the building on two sides does exactly this: complementing the architecture in its geometric proportions, while the planter boxes positioned throughout the water – some sunk beneath the surface, others raised just above it – immediately introduce the Brazilian landscape, great blocks of singly-grouped plants matching the scale of building and water in an effect that could only be achieved with such success in luxuriant tropical conditions.

Burle Marx's landscapes have been created on a large scale and, although much of the work is characterized by intensity of detail, his use of water in combination with dramatic planting, in smaller gardens has enabled him to make simple but effective landscape statements. In one garden an amorphously shaped pool reflects the slender trunk and spreading crown of a Caribbean Royal Palm alongside the contrasting circular leaves of *Victoria amazonica*. In another garden, a river flows out of the surrounding forest and expands into a natural swimming-pool; the planting on the banks maintains complete continuity between forest and garden, the one merging into the other along the water's course.

A third garden, one of Burle Marx's most recent, created between 1984 and 1989, retains a delightful link with the past, having been created on the site of an old coffee plantation. The water which dominates the layout was originally brought from the nearby river to power the plant which processed the coffee beans. It descends in abundance through the garden in three levels from a large natural pond at the top, via two waterfalls to another pool and down to swimming pools on the lowest levels. As in other gardens, Burle Marx used bold groups of plants to emphasize the contrast between the strongly geometric stone walls of the waterfalls and the softer expanse of water in the pool below.

Burle Marx's work has been so widely admired because, while demonstrating how the vision of a painter can be applied to gardens and landscape, it has broken down the age-old opposition of formal and informal, successfully integrating abstract form into gardens and achieving a unity between modern architecture and natural landscape. There is little question that he has been able to do this so forcefully because of the materials at his disposal provided by the tropical climate of Brazil. His example has been followed by gardeners in many other tropical areas of the world.

In Roberto Burle Marx's gardens great expanses of water and vivid planting soften the effect of large-scale Modernist architecture. Such combination of water, planting and architecture was especially evident in his work from 1960 on the landscaping of Brasilia, the new capital city of Brazil; his designs there included one for the garden of the Ministry of Foreign Affairs (above).

In Japan water is integral to both the re-creation of natural scenery, the imagery and the sense of illusion to which all gardens aspire: Shinshui-ai, Kyoto (left) and the Heian Singu shrine garden (below).

Deliberately arranged rocks in water induce a profound sense of peace and tranquillity: Kajujin Temple, Kyoto (above) and Machida, Tokyo (left).

The Oriental Water Garden

It is in China that man's relationship with nature, both philosophical and physical, has been most continuously celebrated in the garden. A tradition stretching back unbroken further than that of any Western country, the creation of gardens in China has been first and foremost an art, inextricably linked to philosophy and religion – the influences of Confucianism, Taoism and, later, Buddhism. It has been closely associated with the arts of the landscape painter and the poet. Indeed, for many centuries nothing ever appeared in a Chinese garden that did not have significance beyond its visual appearance, both individually and as part of an overall scheme. The Chinese garden has always aspired towards Confucius's ideal that 'the wise find joy in water; the benevolent find joy in mountains'. These two elements, water and mountains, often in the reduced form of selected rocks, have always been the essential elements for garden designers whether grand or modest. *Shanshui*, the Chinese word for landscape, means literally 'hills and water'.

The extremes are the great landscapes created by emperors, such as that of the Summer Palace outside Peking, which survived in restored form, and the small private, usually urban, gardens created in far greater numbers, in which the ideals of landscape were realized in microcosm. Regardless of size, however, the designs have been dictated by various considerations: the desire to reproduce a favoured landscape, whether natural or man-made; *yin* and *yang*, the two opposing forces governing all life, with water representing the feminine *yin* in contrast to the masculine *yang*, represented by rocks; and the use of techniques, such as *jie jung* or 'borrowing views', in which elements outside a garden are deliberately incorporated in the overall plan, often to give an appearance of increased size and always to give a picture of harmony with nature.

In the earliest documented dynasty, the Shang, dating from before 1000 BC, the Chinese rulers, like their counterparts in Assyria, enclosed large hunting parks in which they created great lakes, both to enhance the landscape and, no doubt, to form new quarries. The development of Confucianism from the fifth century BC and subsequently Taoism during the third century BC set the attitudes which were to dominate China for centuries thereafter. Indeed, the principles governing Chinese garden design remained remarkably constant, in strict contrast to what was happening in the West. Such change as there was tended to be much more in the form of geographical location with the creation of outstanding gardens reflecting the financial and cultural strength of various cities.

For over two thousand years, from the beginning of the Han dynasty in 206 BC, until the end of the Qing or Manchu dynasty in 1911, Chinese garden-making remained preoccupied with the interrelation of certain primary elements: water, rocks, occasional architectural features such as bridges, pavilions or covered walks with open sides known as *lang*, trees with symbolic significance, in particular the plum, bamboo and pine ('the three friends of winter'), and a limited selection of flowers, including lotus, peonies and chrysanthemums. The grass lawns so favoured in Western gardens, however, had no place.

The use of water in the Chinese garden had both a spiritual significance, in providing a sense of infinity, and a practical role, in creating an impression of the countryside in the garden. Water and mountains and water and islands were the two major harmonies to be expressed in a garden and could be just as effectively achieved with two or three stones and a small pool as with the hundreds of acres of water in the Kunming Lake at the Summer Palace.

The city of Hangzhou, positioned to the south of Shanghai on the edge of the Ch'ien-Tang estuary and established as their capital by the rulers of the Sung dynasty from the early twelfth century, retains perhaps the most important and revered among large Chinese water landscapes. The city lies between the sea and the enormous West Lake, which covers over 1,200 acres and was originally dug during the seventh century. The huge expanse of water, encircled by mountains, is divided into three areas of varying size by dikes; it is bordered by willows and contains a number of man-made islands. Marco Polo described the lake as being the focus for social life and entertainment under the Sung. Similar great expanses of water dominate the major park gardens of Peking, notably the Beihai Park and the Zhonghai and Nanhai. The former underwent constant change from its original creation during the tenth century, but the dominating feature has always been the lake which fills most of the park. Until the early twentieth century the lake of Zhonghai (Central Sea to Beihai's North and Nanhai's Southern Seas) was joined to Beihai by a long sinuous extension with edges close planted with trees which shroud various buildings. The Nanhai, very different in shape from Zhonghai, was the last of the lakes to be dug and dates from the Ming dynasty.

Outside the city of Peking lies the walled Summer Palace; it survives with its lake gardens in the state to which it was restored following damage over a considerable period. The landscape is made the more dramatic by the contrast of, on one side of the palace, the man-made Hill of Longevity descending into the narrow, sinuous back lake and the

Great lakes, natural or man made, and surrounding mountains have for centuries been the classic ingredients of the greatest Chinese gardens. This Western engraving after a Chinese woodcut shows the gardens of the Summer Palace outside Peking.

enormous expanse of the Kunming lake which stretches away to the south of the palace. As at Hangzhou, the lake is divided into three areas of different size by dikes and contains a number of man-made islands. From the palace the view in one direction extends to where the Bridge of the Seventeen Arches crosses from the east side to the island of the Dragon King Temple. On the opposite side of the lake is the Bridge of the Jade Belt, arched in a manner of great significance in Chinese gardens so that the reflection completes a circle or moon shape. Beyond are the Western Hills forming the backdrop to the water. With the various buildings inside the palace and along the lakeside, not least the seemingly endless *lang* stretching for some 2,000 yards along the water's edge, the overall picture is one of great complexity and yet there is also striking simplicity in the form of the lake and mountains beyond.

Probably the most complete of all the large, imperial Chinese landscapes is Bi Shu Shan Zhuang, which has the added quality of mystery derived from its position in a remote area beyond the Great Wall. Indeed, its atmosphere is comparable to the Kashmir havens used by the rulers of India to escape the oppressive heat during the pre-monsoon season. It was created as a retreat in the early eighteenth century by the emperor Kang XI and continued by his successor. Covering thousands of acres, the landscape is dominated by the natural hills that fill most of the area; it falls away in one direction towards a group of lakes which are fed by water from hot springs and which fill much of the park created as a setting for the palace buildings. In the traditional manner the lakes are divided by dikes and scattered with small islands on which stand towers and pavilions and which were the destinations for boating expeditions celebrating the peaceful quality of the landscape.

Quite different in scale to the great imperial landscapes were the gardens of the city of Suzhou, of which a select number survive in restored form. Yet, in this city sometimes referred to as 'the Venice of the East', the central importance of water is if anything more evident. This is nowhere more amply demonstrated than in the garden of Zhuo Zheng Yuan which was begun under the Ming dynasty in the early sixteenth century and given subsequent additions.

A number of fundamental attitudes towards gardening passed from China to Japan, with the result that, while the appearance and style of individual gardens was noticeably different, many of the aspirations behind their creation were similar. Garden design in Japan did not really begin in any recognizable form until the Heian period, which lasted from

This intimate, enclosed water garden in the Chinese city of Suzhou gives a strong indication why it is often called the 'Venice of the East'.

This 'Japanese' garden (opposite) is in fact at Coombe Wood, Surrey, and is Edwardian, demonstrating the fascination which the delicate art of the Eastern water garden has always held for Westerners. The combination of quiet water and bridge seems to evoke an entirely authentic sense of peace and union with the natural world.

One of the most enduring images of the Japanese garden and its use of water is the temple and its reflection seemingly floating in an ethereal world; this example is the Kinkaku-ji, or Golden Temple, at Kyoto.

the eighth century until the end of the twelfth century. By this time, the chief influences were native Japanese Shintoism, imported Chinese culture and the Buddhist religion. This ensured that Japanese gardens like their Chinese counterparts evolved primarily from veneration for nature and tended towards a contemplative rather than a social or festive atmosphere.

The twin essentials of the Japanese garden have been, from the earliest period, water and rocks, a relationship that has been extended to the extremes of the dry garden, originally created by Zen Buddhist monks, in which water is represented by raked sand. The far larger stroll gardens are characterized by an appointed path which winds around a landscape of lake, streams and hills embellished with buildings, trees and flowers.

Through the successive periods of Japanese gardens their overall appearance and the details of their water features have been governed by fixed principles. As a result any educated Japanese person has immediately been able to appreciate and feel in harmony with the hidden meanings which so baffle the European mind. From the Heian period came the tradition that a garden's lake or pond should be shaped like a flying crane and the main island like a tortoise – both bird and animal symbolizing longevity. Otherwise, a lake might be shaped like the Japanese character for 'spirit'. Waterfalls have always been among the most admired of all natural features and wherever possible were introduced into gardens. Where available space did not permit the deployment of large quantities of water, then an arrangement of stones and sand could convey the idea. Ideally, the waterfall was positioned at the edge of a garden, giving the allusion of a constant source of water behind, and where the water flowed on through a garden its course was inevitably from east to west, curving along the way towards the south and winding through numerous smaller bends and twists that disguised its full extent.

The introduction during the sixteenth century and subsequent importance of the tea ceremony brought its own particular characteristics to Japanese gardens: tangible in the form of the necessary water-basin and lantern and the tea-house itself; symbolic in the need for seclusion. Equally full of illusion and representation have been level gardens, often created in small spaces which do not allow for a garden containing the physical representations of nature.

The level garden was raised to a peak of contemplative simplicity in the Zen gardens, of which Ryoan-ji in Kyoto is the supreme example. A rectangle of raked quartz contains fifteen rocks in seemingly disparate but mathematically harmonious groups. The presence of water is only alluded to, whereas at Daisen-in, also in Kyoto, probably the second most important surviving Zen garden, the presence of water is far more clearly represented.

Perhaps the most enduring images of the Japanese water garden are the vision of a pavilion seen across the waters of a lake or pond and the stroll garden gradually unveiling itself to the visitor. The majority of such gardens to survive are in Kyoto, the capital city from 793 until 1868 and the centre of Japanese gardening design. The most important model for Japanese garden pavilions was built in the fourteenth-century Saiho-ji garden and survives most famously in the restored Golden Pavilion, Kinkaku-ji, originally built in the later fourteenth century and restored after being damaged by fire in 1950, and the smaller, fifteenth-century Silver Pavilion, Ginkaku-ji. Both pavilions are in the same architectural style and are positioned in their gardens as if surrounded by water. The verandahs along the temples' various sides offer contrasting views across the lakes, to islands or the water's edge shrouded in trees.

The stroll gardens, which came later, incorporated many of the traditions of earlier gardens; the two outstanding examples are the Katura Imperial Villa and the Shaguku-in Imperial Villa, both dating from the seventeenth century. The former is completely hidden by trees and self-contained, focusing upon the central irregular lake around and across which its set path of 1,760 stones winds to link the various islands, inlets and buildings, such as the tea-house and temple, and to reveal the garden as a succession of views across the water. An exceptional feature of Shaguku-in is that, from the uppermost of the garden's three villas, the lake which forms the focal point of the stroll garden also provides the foreground for the *shakkei* or 'borrowed view', as in Chinese garden design, which extends across Kyoto to the distant hills.

*A*nother image of Japanese garden design, which Western gardeners have always found particularly attractive, is the symbolic dry garden, in which water is represented by raked pebbles, a recognition of the timeless world of nature captured in the garden.

Bibliography

ACTON, Harold, *The Villas of Tuscany*, London, 1973.

BARDI, P.M., *The Tropical Gardens of Roberto Burle Marx*, London, 1964.

BERRALL, Julia S., *The Garden*, London, 1966.

BLOMFIELD, Reginald and Thomas, F. Inigo, *The Formal Garden in England*, London, 1892.

BRACKENHOFFER, Elie, *Voyage de Paris en Italie 1644–46*, trans. Henry Lehr, 1927.

BROOKES, John, *Garden Design Book*, London, 1991.

BROOKES, John, *Gardens of Paradise*, London, 1987.

BROWN, Jane, *The English Garden in Our Time*, 1987.

BROWN, Jane, *Gardens of a Golden Afternoon*, London, 1982.

CAMPBELL, Craig, S., *Water in Landscape Architecture*, New York, 1978.

CLIFFORD, Derek, *A History of Garden Design*, London, 1962.

CROWE, Sylvia, *Garden Design*, London, 1962.

DE CASA VALDÉS, Marquess, *Spanish Gardens*, Woodbridge, Suffolk, 1987.

DE CAUS, Salomon, *Les raisons des forces mouvantes*, London, 1615.

DEZALLIER D'ARGENVILLE, Antoine-Joseph, *La théorie et la pratique du jardinage* (The Theory and Practice of Gardening), trans. John James, London, 1712.

ECKBO, Garrett, *Landscape for Living*, New York, 1950.

ELIOVSON, Sima, *The Gardens of Roberto Burle Marx*, London, 1991.

ELLIOTT, Brent, *Victorian Gardens*, London, 1986.

GOTHEIN, Marie Luise, *A History of Garden Art*, 2 vols., trans. Laura Archer Hind, New York, 1928.

HADFIELD, Miles, *et al.*, *British Gardeners, A Biographical Dictionary*, London, 1980.

HADFIELD, Miles, *Gardening in Britain*, London, 1960.

HUNT, J.D., *William Kent*, London, 1987.

HUNT, Peter (ed.), *The Book of Garden Ornament*, London, 1974.

HUSSEY, Christopher, *English Gardens and Landscapes 1700–1750*, London, 1967.

HUSSEY, Christopher, *The Picturesque*, London, 1927.

HYAMS, Edward, *A History of Gardens and Gardening*, London, 1971.

HYAMS, Edward, *Capability Brown and Humphry Repton*, London, 1971.

JEKYLL, Gertrude, *Wood and Garden*, London, 1899.

JELLICOE, Geoffrey, *The Guelph Lectures on Landscape Design*, Guelph, Ont., 1983.

JELLICOE, Geoffrey and Susan, *The Landscape of Man*, London, 1975.

JELLICOE, Geoffrey and Susan, *The Use of Water in Landscape Architecture*, London, 1971.

JELLICOE, Geoffrey and Susan *et al.*, *The Oxford Companion to Gardens*, London, 1986.

JONES, Barbara, *Follies and Grottoes*, London, 1979.

KARSON, Robin, *Fletcher Steele, Landscape Architect*, New York, 1989.

KESWICK, Maggie, *The Chinese Garden, Art, History and Architecture*, London, 1978.

KIMBALL, Hubbard and Theodora, *An Introduction to the Study of Landscape Design*, New York, 1917.

KUCK, Lorraine, *The World of the Japanese Garden*, New York, 1972.

LEHRMAN, Jonas, *Earthly Paradise*, London, 1980.

LYALL, Sutherland, *Designing the New Landscape*, London, 1991.

McGUIRE, Diane Kostial, *Gardens of America: Three Centuries of Design*, Charlottesville, 1989.

MAWSON, Thomas, *The Art and Craft of Garden Making*, London, 1990.

MASSON, Georgina, *Italian Gardens*, London, 1961.

MONTAIGNE, Michel Eyquem [de], *Journal de voyage en Italie*, trans. E.J. Trechmann, 1929.

MOSSER, Monique and Teyssot, Georges (eds.), *The History of Garden Design*, London, 1991.

Acknowledgments

MOYNIHAN, Elizabeth B., *Paradise as a Garden in Persia and Mughal India*, London, 1980.

OLDHAM, J. and R., *Gardens in Time*, Sydney, 1980.

OTTEWELL, David, *The Edwardian Garden*, London, 1989.

PAGE, Russell, *The Education of a Gardener*, London, 1962.

PLINY THE YOUNGER, *Letters* (trans. Betty Radice), London, 1963.

RAY, Helen Mary and Nicholls, Robert P., *A Guide to Significant and Historic Gardens of the USA*, New York, 1982.

ROPER, Laura, *A Biography of Frederick Law Olmsted*, New York, 1973.

SCHINZ, Marina and Gabrielle van Zuylen, *The Gardens of Russell Page*, New York, 1991.

SHEPHERD, J.C. and Jellicoe, Geoffrey, *Italian Gardens of the Renaissance*, London, 1986.

SITWELL, Sir George, *On the Making of Gardens*, London, 1909.

STONE, Doris M., *The Great Public Gardens of the Eastern USA*, New York, 1982.

STRONG, Roy, *The Renaissance Garden in England*, London, 1979.

STROUD, Dorothy, *Capability Brown*, London, 1950.

THACKER, Christopher, *The History of Gardens*, London, 1979.

TRIGG, H. Inigo, *Garden Craft in Europe*, London, 1913.

TURNER, Tom, *English Garden Design*, Woodbridge, 1986.

WALPOLE, Horace, *On Modern Gardening*, London, 1785.

WARREN, William, *The Tropical Garden*, London, 1991.

WATKIN, David, *The English Vision*, London, 1982.

WHARTON, Edith, *Italian Villas and their Gardens*, New York, 1903.

WILSON, Michael, *William Kent*, London, 1984.

WOODBRIDGE, Keneneth, *Princely Gardens*, London, 1986.

The author, photographer and publishers would like to thank all those owners of water gardens around the world who helped the production of this book with information and permission to visit or photograph their gardens.

Illustration Acknowledgments

Black and white illustrations

Photo Alinari 51, 55; Aleppo Museum 19; Bedfordshire Record Office (Lord Lucas Collection, BRO L 33/208) 150; Besançon, Musée des Beaux-Arts et d'Archéologie (photo Bulloz) 63; photo G. Careaga 95 r; Devonshire Collection, Chatsworth. Reproduced by permission of the Chatsworth Settlement Trustees 194; Florence, Museo di Firenze com'era (photo Soprintendenza alle Gallerie) 58 t; Lawrence Halprin Associates (photo Lawrence Halprin) 166 r; photo Martin Hürlimann 203; Kassel, Staatliche Kunstsammlungen 103; photo A. F. Kersting 115 r; Office of Dan Kiley 167; photo S. Jellicoe 95 l, 158, 202; photo Jonas Lehrman 24, 36, 37, 38 t, 38 b, 39; London, Austrian National Tourist Office 71; British Museum 18, 67 l; Victoria and Albert Museum 35, 98; photo Ian Mackenzie-Kerr 94; photo Georgina Masson 22, 62 t; Dr Roberto Burle Marx 166 l, 195; New York, The Metropolitan Museum of Art 17; Novosti Press Agency 99; photo Hugh Palmer 34, 42, 43, 54, 58 b, 59 t, 59 b, 66 t, 66 b, 70, 83, 86, 88, 102, 106, 107 t, 107 b, 111, 118, 119 r, 119 l, 186, 187, 190; Paris, Bibliothèque Nationale 50, 77 b, 81 t, 82, 84, 87 t, 91, 199; Colin Penn 201; Philadelphia, Philadelphia Museum of Art 21; Private Collection (photo *Country Life*) 110; Rousham Collections (photo Courtauld Institute of Art, University of London) 146; photo Marina Schinz 191; Musée de Versailles (photo Réunion des Musées Nationaux, Paris) 81 b; photo Alexander Zielcke 67 r.

All colour photographs in this book are by Hugh Palmer, except the following: Japanese National Tourist Organization 197 t; Geoffrey Jellicoe 164, 165; Jonas Lehrman 8 l, 40, 41, 45 b; Luca Invernizzi Tettoni 192, 193; Bill Tingey 8 r, 196, 197 b.

Famous Water Gardens

In addition to gardens where water is the primary factor, the list below includes gardens with major water features. It also includes a few cases where a city's name, such as Pompeii or Isfahan, covers a quantity of different gardens. The list only includes gardens or water features that are still substantially intact today; those that have completely disappeared are not listed. The order of listing corresponds as closely as possible to the order of chapters in the main body of the book.

Rome and Persia
Hadrian's Villa, *Tivoli, Italy*.
Isfahan, *Iran*.
Pompeii, *Italy*.

Spain
Alcazar Palace, *Seville*.
Alhambra, *Granada*.
Aranjuez, *Madrid*.
Generalife, *Granada*.
La Granja, *Segovia*.
Patio de los Naranjos, *Cordoba*.

India, Pakistan and Kashmir
Achabal, *Islamabad, Kashmir*.
Humayan, *Delhi, India*.
Nishat Bagh, *Srinigar, Kashmir*.
Ram Bagh, *Agra, India*.
Shahdara, *Lahore, Pakistan*.
Shalamar Bagh, *Lahore, Pakistan*.
Shalamar Bagh, *Srinigar, Kashmir*.
Taj Mahal, *Agra, India*.
Vernag, *Islamabad, Kashmir*.

Italy
Boboli Gardens, *Florence*.
Isolo Bella, *Lake Maggiore*.
Palazzo Farnese, *Caprarola*.
Palazzo Reale, *Caserta*.

Villa Aldobrandini, *Frascati*.
Villa Cigogna, *Bisuschio*.
Villa d'Este, *Tivoli*.
Villa Gamberaia, *Settignano*.
Villa Garzoni, *Collodi*.
Villa Lante, *Bagnaia*.
Villa Marlia, *Lucca*.
Villa Pisani, *Strà*.

France
Chantilly, *Oise*.
Chenonceaux, *Indre-et-Loire*.
Courances, *Essonne*.
Dampière, *Yvelines*.
Ermenonville, *Oise*.
Fontainebleau, *Seine-et-Marne*.
Giverny, *Eure*.
Maintenon, *Eure-et-Loir*.
Saint-Cloud, *Hauts-de-Seine*.
Sceaux, *Hauts-de-Seine*.
Vaux-le-Vicomte, *Seine-et-Marne*.
Versailles, *Yvelines*.

The Netherlands and Germany
Herrenhausen, *Hanover, Germany*.
Het Loo, *Apeldoorn, Netherlands*.
Nymphenburg, *Bavaria, Germany*.
Schleissheim, *Bavaria, Germany*.
Schwetzingen, *Baden-Würtemberg, Germany*.
Seist, *Utrecht, Netherlands*.
Wilhelmshöhe, *Hesse, Germany*.
Wörlitz, *Halle, Germany*.

United Kingdom and Ireland
An Cala, *Argyllshire*.
Anne's Grove, *County Cork*.
Arbigland House, *Dumfries and Galloway*.
Arduaine, *Strathclyde*.
Athelhampton Manor, *Dorset*.
Birr Castle, *County Offaly*.
Blenheim Palace, *Oxfordshire*.

Bodnant, *Gwynedd*.
Bramham Park, *Yorkshire*.
Buscot Park, *Oxfordshire*.
Castle Ward, *County Down*.
Chatsworth, *Derbyshire*.
Chillington, *West Midlands*.
Compton Acres, *Dorset*.
Crarae Lodge, *Argyllshire*.
Dunrobin Castle, *Sutherland*.
Dyffryn, *Glamorgan*.
Erdigg, *Clwyd*.
Folly Farm, *Berkshire*.
Heale House, *Wiltshire*.
Hodnet Hall, *Shropshire*.
Kildrummy Castle, *Grampian*.
Logan Botanic Garden, *Dumfries and Galloway*.
Longstock, *Hampshire*
Muckross House, *County Kerry*.
Penrhyn Castle, *Gwynedd*.
Powerscourt, *County Wicklow*.
Rousham House, *Oxfordshire*.
Sezincote, *Gloucestershire*.
Shute House, *Wiltshire*.
Stourhead, *Wiltshire*.
Studley Royal, *Yorkshire*.
Tully House Japanese Garden, *County Kildare*.
Tyringham, *Buckinghamshire*.
Warbrook House, *Hampshire*.
Westbury Court, *Gloucestershire*.
West Wycombe Park, *Buckinghamshire*.
Wrest Park, *Hertfordshire*.

Austria, Hungary, Czechoslovakia, Poland and Russia
Arkadia, *Poland*.
Buchlovice, *South Moravia, Czechoslovakia*.
Lazienki Park, *Warsaw, Poland*.
Lednice, *South Moravia, Czechoslovakia*.
Martonvasar, *Hungary*.
Pavlovsk, *St. Petersburg, Russia*.
Peterhof, *St. Petersburg, Russia*.

Pruhonice Park, *Prague, Czechoslovakia*.
Schönbrunn, *Vienna, Austria*.
Tata, *Hungary*.
Tsarskoe Selo, *St. Petersburg, Russia*.

United States
Biltmore House, *North Carolina*.
Boston Park System, *Massachussetts*.
Dumbarton Oaks, *Washington DC*.
El Novillero, *California*.
Falling Water, *Pennsylvania*.
Filoli, *California*.
Fountain Plaza, *Dallas, Texas*.
Frick Museum, *New York*.
Hearst Gardens, *San Simeon, California*.
Longwood, *Pennsylvania*.
Lovejoy Plaza, *Portland, Oregon*.
Meadowbank Farm, *Pennsylvania*.
Mount Cuba, *Delaware*.
Naumkeag, *Massachussetts*.
Nemours, *Delaware*.
PepsiCo Park, *New York*.
Phillips House, *California*.
Vizcaya, *Florida*.
William Paca Garden, *Maryland*.

China and Japan
Beihai Park, *Peking, China*.
Bi Shu Shan Zhuang, *Chengde, China*.
Daisen-in, *Kyoto, Japan*.
Ginkaku-ji, *Kyoto, Japan*.
Katsura Imperial Villa, *Kyoto, Japan*.
Kinkaku-ji, *Kyoto, Japan*.
Nanhai, *Peking, China*.
Saiho-ji, *Kyoto, Japan*.
Shi Zi Lin, *Suzhou, China*.
Shugaku-in Imperial Villa, *Kyoto, Japan*.
Wang Shi Yuan, *Suzhou, China*.
Xi Hu, *Hangzhou, China*.
Yi He Yuan (Summer Palace), *Peking, China*.
Yi Yuan, *Suzhou, China*.
Zhonghai, *Peking, China*.

Index

Bold numerals indicate illustrations